Presented to:

....

From:

....

Date:

....

CLASSIC BEDTIME
Bible Stories
and Devotions
for Kids

Published by Shiloh Kidz, an imprint of Barbour Publishing, Inc., 1810 Barbour Drive, Uhrichsville, Ohio 44683, www.shilohkidz.com

Our mission is to inspire the world with the life-changing message of the Bible.

Member of the
Evangelical Christian
Publishers Association

Printed in China.

06566   0819   DS

CLASSIC
BEDTIME
Bible Stories
and Devotions
for Kids

Inspired by Jesse Lyman Hurlbut's Story of the Bible
with Devotions by Janice Thompson

Illustrated by Alessia Girasole

SHILOH kidz
An Imprint of Barbour Publishing, Inc.

God Creates the Earth

Genesis 1:1–19

The earth is very old. No one knows when it was made. But God has always been alive.

He created the heavens and the earth. The earth was empty and very dark and covered with water. Nothing lived on the earth.

God said, "Let there be light," and there was light. God saw that the light was good. He called the light Day and the darkness Night. This was the first day. On the second day, God spoke and made the sky.

Next God said, "I want the dry land to come out of the water." So it did. God named the land Earth and the waters Sea. God saw that this was good. Then God said, "Let all the green plants grow out of the earth." All this happened on the third day, and it was good.

Then on the fourth day, God spoke again. He said, "Let the sun and moon and stars come into the sky." So this happened. God put them in the sky to give light to the earth. The sun shines in the day. The moon and stars shine at night. God saw that this was good, too.

Nothing Becomes Something

*In the beginning God made from nothing
the heavens and the earth.*
GENESIS 1:1

God made something out of nothing! He spoke to the darkness and the earth was formed. Then He put all kinds of fun things on the earth, like beautiful rivers and snowy mountains and ocean waves that knock you over when you try to stand in them. How did He make all of that from nothing at all? When Mom bakes a cake, she uses flour, eggs, oil, and other ingredients. She mixes them together, puts the batter in a pan, and pops it into the oven until it bakes into a yummy cake you can eat. But when God made the world, He started with nothing at all. He just spoke and things started happening! What an awesome God we serve.

*Lord, You're an amazing Creator!
I'm so happy to be Your kid. Amen.*

God Creates the Earth

GENESIS 1:20–2:3

On the fifth day, God spoke again. He said, "I want the seas to be filled with living things. I want birds to fly in the sky." So God created everything that lives in the sea and flies in the sky. And God blessed them.

Then God said, "Let the animals live on earth." So He created big animals and little things that creep on the ground. God saw that all this was good.

Finally God said, "Now I am going to make human beings. Unlike the animals, they will stand up tall and have a soul. They will be like Me, rule the earth, and care for it." So God took some dust from the ground and formed man. He breathed the breath of life into him. Man became alive.

God blessed them saying, "I want you to live all over the earth." God saw that everything He had made was very good. This ended the sixth day.

On the seventh day, God rested. His work was done. So He blessed that day and made it holy.

Made Like Him

And God made man in His own likeness. In the likeness
of God He made him. He made both male and female.
GENESIS 1:27

We don't know what God looks like, but we do know that we are created in His image. Is He tall? Short? Thin? Chubby? Does He look like an old man with a long white beard and eyes that twinkle when He sees you? Does He have freckles? Does He look like your brother or your dad or your grandpa? No one knows. One day we'll get to see Him in heaven. What a fun surprise it will be when we get to see God face-to-face. For now, you can use your active imagination to think about what He's like.

I'm made in Your image, God! That makes my
heart so happy. I want to be just like You. Amen.

Ādam Lives in the Garden

GENESIS 2:8–24

The man God created was named Adam. God planted a garden in Eden to be Adam's home. This garden was big. Four rivers ran through it. Beautiful plants and trees grew there. They were good for food. God told Adam to take care of the garden.

Next God created the animals and birds out of the dust. He brought them to the man, and Adam named them all. But Adam was alone. "This is not good," God said. "I will make someone to be with Adam and to help him." So God made Eve.

Don't Be Lonely

The Lord God made woman from the bone which He had taken from the man. And He brought her to the man.
GENESIS 2:22

The man God created lived in a beautiful garden, surrounded by trees, rivers, and mountains. But Adam was lonely. There were only monkeys, zebras, and other animals to hang out with. Adam didn't have anyone to talk to. It's hard to have a chat with a parrot or a penguin. Do you know what it's like to be lonely? Do you ever wish you had a special friend? God knew that Adam needed someone, so He made Eve, a woman. Adam must have been very surprised when he woke up from a long nap to discover he had someone to talk to!

Thank You, God, that I don't ever have to be lonely. You'll always be my best friend. Amen.

Eve Is Tricked by the Serpent

GENESIS 2:20–3:7

God made Eve in a wonderful way: When Adam was asleep, God took a rib out of him. God made a woman with that rib and brought her to Adam. They loved each other. Adam named the woman Eve. They lived at peace in their beautiful garden. They cared for it as God asked, and God walked with them there.

Two special trees grew in Eden. One was named the Tree of Life. God warned them about the other tree. It was the Tree of the Knowledge of Good and Evil. "If you eat of this tree," He said, "you will die."

Now there was a sneaky creature in the garden—the serpent. He said to Eve, "Did God say you shouldn't eat the Tree of Knowledge?" Eve answered, "He said if we do we will die."

"That is not true," the serpent lied. "Eat it and you will be like God." Eve believed him and ate the tree's fruit. She gave some to Adam and he ate it. Suddenly, they knew they were wrong. For the first time they were afraid to meet God.

Don't Fall for the Devil's Tricks

*Now the snake was more able to fool others than
any animal of the field which the Lord God had made.
He said to the woman, "Did God say that you should
not eat from any tree in the garden?"*
GENESIS 3:1

That snake was so tricky! He tried to get Eve to do the wrong thing, and she fell right into his trap! Because of her mistake, Adam and Eve got kicked out of the garden forever. Wow, God took that mistake seriously, didn't He? Some people are like that snake. They're naughty and they want you to be naughty, too. But you know better. You won't fall into the trap like Eve did. When someone says, "Let's eat more cookies, even though Mom said we couldn't," you say, "No thanks!" because you know better.

I want to make good choices, Lord. Please help me. Amen.

Adam and Eve Leave the Garden

GENESIS 3:8–24

God walked in the cool garden breeze. But Adam and Eve were hiding among the trees. "Where are you?" called God. "I heard you and was afraid," the man answered. "So I hid from you."

"Did you eat from the tree I warned you about?" asked God.

"The woman gave me the fruit. I ate it," the man said. So God spoke to the woman. "What have you done?"

"The serpent tricked me," she said, "and I ate." God turned to the serpent. "You have done this, so you will always crawl on your belly. You will hate the woman. She will also hate you. You and her child will fight. He will crush your head. You will bite him on the heel."

Then God told the woman, "You will have children. But you will be in pain when you do."

"Adam," God said, "you listened to her and ate from the tree. So you must work for all you get from the earth. You will sweat and suffer all your life. I made you out of dust. So you will turn back into dust."

Then God sent them out of the garden.

We All Make Mistakes

Then they heard the sound of the Lord God
walking in the garden in the evening. The man
and his wife hid themselves from the Lord
God among the trees of the garden.
GENESIS 3:8

Oops! Adam and Eve made a big mistake! They disobeyed God and then tried to hide from Him. He found them, of course. God is pretty good at hide-and-seek. Adam and Eve had to be disciplined for their bad choices. Have you ever disobeyed your parents? What happened? Did you have to take a time-out? Were you sent to your room? Did Mom take away your favorite toy or make you skip dessert? We all make mistakes. Every single person messes up. But God loves us, and He forgives us when we ask Him to.

Lord, I've made a lot of mistakes. Thank You
for forgiving me when I mess up. Amen.

Cain Murders His Brother

GENESIS 3:23–4:16

Adam and Eve lived outside the garden until they died. A flaming sword guards the path to the Tree of Life. No one has gone back there since they left.

Eve gave birth to a baby boy named Cain. Her second baby was a boy named Abel.

When the boys became men, they worked like their father. Cain was a farmer. Abel was a shepherd. One day Cain brought fruit to give to God. He worked to grow the fruit on his farm. Abel had a gift for God, too. He gave a lamb that had been born in the field. God was happy with Abel's gift. But He refused Cain's gift.

Cain became angry, so God asked him, "Why are you angry? Be careful. Sin might catch you." Later, Cain killed Abel while he was walking in the field. God asked Cain, "Where is your brother?"

"I don't know," Cain answered. "Should I care for my brother?"

"What have you done?" God said. "Listen, Abel's blood is crying to Me from the ground. You murdered Abel. You will always live under a curse."

So Cain went away from God. He lived east of Eden in the land of Nod.

Brothers and Sisters

Then the Lord said to Cain, "Why are you angry?
And why are you looking down?"
GENESIS 4:6

Brothers and sisters don't always get along, do they? Sometimes they fight and squabble because they think Mom or Dad likes the other one better. That's what happened with Cain and Abel. Cain got jealous because he thought Abel was God's favorite. The truth is, God loves all of us the same, no matter how big or small we are. He doesn't care if we have freckles, messy hair, or mismatched socks. He's not worried about whether we're the youngest or the oldest, the tallest or the shortest. He loves each of us to the moon and back. So don't get jealous. Remember, God loves you.

I'm glad we are all Your favorites, God.
I feel happy knowing You love us all the same. Amen.

Noah Builds the Ark

GENESIS 6:1–8:19

A long time passed after Cain killed Abel. The land was full of people. God looked at the world He had made. The people were wicked. God said, "I am sorry I made these people."

But God saw one good man named Noah. He told Noah, "I am going to wipe out the people I made. They will die with all things on earth. Only you are living right. So you and your family will be saved." Then God told Noah to build a huge boat called an ark. This ark was as big as a three-story building. "I am going to flood the earth with water," God said. "All the people and all the animals will drown."

"Noah," God went on, "bring two of every kind of animal into the ark. Gather food for them and for yourself. Then go into the ark with your family. In seven days I will send rain. The rain will fall for forty days. Everything I created will be wiped off the earth." And Noah did all the things God told him to do. Noah was six hundred years old when the rain started. Rain fell for forty days and forty nights. It rained like windows in the sky were opened.

One Good Man

But Noah found favor in the eyes of the Lord.
GENESIS 6:8

Oh boy, this is a tough one! Almost everyone was doing wrong. God couldn't seem to find anyone who would obey Him. He searched and searched until He found one good man, Noah. God was proud of Noah for doing what was right and sent him on an adventure in a big boat called an ark. God is always happy when He sees people doing the right thing. He loves to reward people. Have you ever been rewarded for obeying? Sometimes it's hard to be the only one living carefully when others around you are doing whatever they want, but you can do it! Keep obeying God and your parents, and you'll get to have a few fun adventures of your own!

I'll keep doing the right thing, Lord.
I want to go on adventures with You. Amen.

The Rainbow of God's Promise

GENESIS 8:20–9:17

The flood was over. Every living thing on earth was killed. Only the animals and people in the ark came through alive. Noah knew what he should do first. He built an altar and gave gifts to God. This way Noah thanked God for saving his family.

God made a promise: "Never again will a flood destroy all life. The four seasons will come and go forever. The earth is yours, Noah. Rule it well."

Suddenly, the first rainbow curved through the sky. Now every time there is a rainbow, people remember God's promise to Noah.

God Always Keeps His Promises

*"I will set My rain-bow in the cloud, and it will be something special
to see because of an agreement between Me and the earth."*
GENESIS 9:13

Drip, drip, drip! Plop, plop, plop! Noah was probably tired of all that rain. When he finally stepped off the ark, God said, "Look up, Noah!" Way up high, in a beautiful blue sky, Noah saw something amazing: a beautiful rainbow with brilliant colors—red, orange, yellow, green, blue, and purple. Have you ever seen a rainbow in the sky? Sometimes you can see one after a big storm. The colorful rainbow is a promise from God that He won't ever destroy the earth with floodwaters again. God is a promise keeper. What about you? Can you keep a promise?

*Lord, thanks for Your promise! I'm going to do
my best to keep my promises, too. Amen.*

Sarah Laughs at God

GENESIS 18:1–21:14

It was a hot day by the oaks of Mamre. Abraham was sitting in the shade near his tent. Looking up, he saw God and two angels standing nearby. They looked just like men. Abraham and his wife, Sarah, rushed to make lunch for them.

"Where is your wife?" God asked. "She is going to have a child soon." In the tent, Sarah heard this and laughed. She was much too old to have children. "Why does she laugh?" God asked. "Nothing is too difficult for Me. At the right time, she will have a baby."

When Abraham was one hundred years old, God kept His promise. Sarah gave birth to a baby boy. They were very happy and had a big feast. They named their son Isaac. His name means "laughing," because Sarah had laughed at God. And Sarah said, "God has brought laughter for me. Everyone who hears will laugh with me."

Be a Promise Keeper

*Sarah was able to have a child and she gave birth to a son
when Abraham was very old. He was born at the
time the Lord said it would happen.*
GENESIS 21:2

S arah couldn't help but laugh when God said she was going to have a baby. After all, she was an old lady! But God always keeps His promises. If He says He will do something, He will do it! What about you? Do you do the things you promise? If you say, "Mom, I'll clean up my room after I'm done playing," do you do it? If you say, "I promise not to be mean to my sister next time," do you remember? God loves when we do what we say.

*Lord, I want to be a promise keeper like You.
The next time I say I'll do something. . .I'll do it! Amen.*

Abraham Offers Isaac to God

GENESIS 22:1–19

Meanwhile, God spoke to Abraham: "Take Isaac and go to Mount Moriah." Abraham loved Isaac. "There," God went on, "slay Isaac as a gift to Me."

Abraham obeyed. They traveled three days to the mountain. Abraham put Isaac on an altar. Isaac asked, "Where is the lamb for God's gift?"

"God will give us a lamb," Abraham answered. He raised the knife to slay his son. Then God's angel stopped him: "I know you fear God. You'd slay your only son for Him." Abraham saw a ram for God's gift stuck in a bush. So Isaac lived.

You Can Trust God

God said, "Take now your son, your only son, Isaac, whom you love.
And go to the land of Moriah. Give him as a burnt gift on the altar
in worship, on one of the mountains I will show you."
GENESIS 22:2

Abraham and Sarah had waited a long time to have their baby boy, Isaac. They were so excited. Then God said, "Give Isaac back to Me as a gift." This made no sense to Abraham, but he trusted that God must have a better plan, so he obeyed. God decided to surprise Abraham, and the story had a happy ending. Sometimes God asks us to do things that seem impossible. We can't figure it out. But when we obey Him, He always surprises us with happy endings.

God, I'm so glad I can trust You for a happy ending.
I want to have the faith that Abraham did. Amen.

Esau Sells His Birthright

GENESIS 25:21–34

Like his father, Abraham, Isaac lived in the land of Canaan. His wife, Rebekah, could not have children. So Isaac prayed, and God answered his prayer. Rebekah gave birth to twin boys. She named them Esau and Jacob.

Esau was born first. He would get twice as much as Jacob when Isaac died. This was called the birthright.

Jacob grew to be a quiet man, living in the tents. Esau became a hunter in the fields. When Esau brought meat from the hunt, he gave some to Isaac. So Isaac loved Esau more than Jacob. But Rebekah liked the wise and careful Jacob.

One day Esau came in from the fields hungry and tired. Since it was time for dinner, Jacob cooked a pot of soup. "Please give me some soup," Esau said.

"Will you trade your birthright for some soup?" Jacob asked.

"Why not?" answered Esau. "I am about to die of hunger. If I do die, I won't need my birthright." And Esau promised Jacob his birthright.

Jacob was selfish with Esau. This was not right. But Esau was foolish to sell his birthright. This was wrong.

Let's Make a Deal

As Jacob was getting food ready one day,
Esau came in from the field and was very hungry.
GENESIS 25:29

Jacob and Esau were twin brothers, but they were very different. One was a hunter and outdoorsman. The other one liked to stay close to home. Like all brothers, they made mistakes at times. Esau made a big one when he sold his birthright. He regretted it later. Do you have brothers or sisters? How are they different from you? How are they similar? Sometimes we make deals with them—"If you clean my room, I'll eat your broccoli." "If you don't tell Mom I broke the lamp, I won't tell her you ate those cookies." Only one problem: making deals usually doesn't end well!

Lord, I love my family, but I'm kind of glad I'm different from
the others. Thanks for loving me just as I am. Amen.

God Wrestles with Jacob

GENESIS 32:24–32

While he was alone, a man grabbed Jacob, and they wrestled until dawn. When he could not win, the man broke Jacob's hip.

"Let me go," the man said.

"I won't let you go unless you bless me," replied Jacob.

"What is your name?"

"Jacob."

"Not anymore," the man said. "It's now Israel."

"Why?" asked Jacob.

"You've wrestled with God and have won."

Then Jacob asked him, "What is your name?" The man only answered, "Why do you want to know?" Then he blessed Jacob.

Jacob said, "I've seen God's face and have lived."

Spend Time with God

And the man said, "Your name will no longer be Jacob, but Israel.
For you have fought with God and with men, and have won."
GENESIS 32:28

Fighting is no fun! When you fight with a friend or your brother or sister, things never end well. In this story, a man named Jacob got into a wrestling match with God. Wow! When Jacob won the fight, God said, "I'm going to change your name to Israel." Why do you suppose God changed his name? When we spend time with God, He changes our name, too! He calls us "Christian," which means "believer in Jesus." He wants us to remember that we are like His Son, Jesus. Isn't it wonderful to be called a Christian?

I want to be like You, Jesus!
Thanks for calling me a Christian. Amen.

Joseph the Dreamer

Genesis 37:1–11

Jacob made peace with Esau and returned to Canaan. Soon another child, named Benjamin, was born to Rachel, Jacob's wife. But Jacob mourned because his lovely Rachel died.

Of all his sons, Jacob loved Joseph best. He rewarded Joseph with a beautiful coat of many colors. Joseph's brothers were jealous. They wished they could have such a coat.

One day Joseph said to his brothers, "Listen to the dreams I've had." When Joseph told them the dreams, his brothers knew their meaning: they would someday bow down to Joseph. The brothers hated Joseph because of his dreams.

Don't Be Jealous

*Now Israel loved Joseph more than all his sons, because Joseph
was born when he was an old man. And Israel made
him a long coat of many colors.*
GENESIS 37:3

Joseph loved to brag because his dad loved him the most. His father gave him a special colorful coat. His brothers were so jealous! Do you blame them? How would you feel if your mom played favorites and loved your brother or sister more than you? That would stink! Sometimes people do play favorites—teachers, friends, even grandparents or siblings. It's no fun feeling like you're being overlooked. But God never overlooks you. He loves you as much as every other kid on the planet.

*I won't be jealous, Lord, even if people don't pay attention
to me. I'll love them no matter what. Amen.*

The Dreamer Is Sold as a Slave

GENESIS 37:12–40:22

Joseph's brothers stole his pretty coat and threw him in a pit. Then they sold him into slavery for twenty silver pieces. Joseph's new owners took him to Egypt.

Joseph's father, Jacob, was so sad. "The boy is gone; what shall I do?"

The brothers decided to lie to Jacob. They stained Joseph's coat with animal blood. Jacob thought Joseph was killed.

"I will weep for my son the rest of my life," Jacob cried.

The caravan carried Joseph south to Egypt, and a man named Potiphar bought Joseph. This man was a leader in Egypt's army.

God was with Joseph, though he was a slave. Potiphar saw his good work and liked him. He put Joseph in charge of his whole house.

Hurting Others Hurts Us

*"Come, let us sell him to the Ishmaelites and not lay our hands
on him. For he is our brother, our own flesh."*
GENESIS 37:27

Joseph's bragging got him in trouble with his brothers. They got so mad at him they decided to throw him in a pit, then sold him to some people passing by. Talk about mean! We all get into fights with family members and friends, but doing mean things is never a good idea. When we hurt others, we end up hurting ourselves, too. God's heart breaks when we fight and squabble. Is there someone you fight with a lot? Have you ever hurt this person? If so, say "I'm sorry!" and try not to do it again. Ask for God's help. He wants you to love others.

*Lord, I'm sorry for the times I've been mad at people.
Please forgive me and help me to do better next time. Amen.*

Jacob's Sons Visit Joseph

GENESIS 42:6-24

Now, as in Joseph's boyhood dreams, his brothers bowed before him. "Who are you?" Joseph asked. "Where do you come from?"

"We've come from Canaan to buy food," they answered.

"No, you didn't," Joseph said. "You're spies. You want to see how weak Egypt has become."

"No, sir. We are twelve brothers," they said. "The youngest is at home. One has died."

"You must prove you aren't spies," Joseph answered. "Someone must go back and bring your youngest brother here." Then the rest were locked up.

Three days later, Joseph spoke: "One of you must remain. The others may leave with your family's food. But bring your youngest brother back to me. Then I'll know you're not spies." The youngest brother, Benjamin, was Rachel's son, like Joseph.

Joseph chose Simeon to stay in Egypt. Reuben told the others, "This has happened because of what you did to Joseph." They didn't know Joseph overheard them. He went away and wept. He knew his brothers were sorry for what they had done.

Making Up Is Fun

They said to one another, "For sure we are guilty for what we did to our brother. We saw the suffering of his soul while he begged us. But we would not listen. So this trouble has come to us."
GENESIS 42:21

❧

Can you imagine being away from your family for a long time? You would miss them, wouldn't you? If you couldn't see your mom or talk to your brother or sister, you would be so sad. That's what happened to Joseph. He was separated from his father and his brothers. But God did a miracle. He brought them all back together. God loves when people make up after an argument or a fight. Sure, everyone experiences conflict now and then, but making up can be a ton of fun!

❧

Lord, sometimes I have a real temper! But You calm me down and help me make up with people I've hurt. Thank You, Lord. Amen.

Moses Is Saved from Death

EXODUS 2:1–10

A baby boy was born in Goshen. His mother saw that he was a fine boy. She hid him from the Egyptians for three months. When she couldn't hide him any longer, she wove a basket. It was made so no water could leak into it. She put the boy in the basket. Then she floated it among the reeds by the river.

Pharaoh's daughter bathed in the river at that place. She discovered the basket and felt sorry for the crying baby. She kept him and named him Moses.

God Watches Over You

Then the daughter of Pharaoh came to wash herself in the Nile. Her young women walked beside the Nile. She saw the basket in the tall grass and sent the woman who served her to get it.
EXODUS 2:5

Can you imagine finding a baby in a river? Wow! That's what happened to this girl, the daughter of the king of Egypt. She found the tiny infant floating in a basket in the river and she saved him. Then she took him to the palace and raised him as her own child. God really protected Moses, didn't He? He protects you, too! He watches over you from the time you're a baby until you grow old. You're never out of His sight. That's how much He cares about you!

Thanks for taking such good care of me, Lord. I know You've protected me, and that makes me happy! Amen.

A Prince Becomes a Shepherd

EXODUS 2:11–25

Moses grew up in Pharaoh's palace. There he learned all the
wisdom of Egypt. He did powerful deeds. But he loved his own
people, Israel. They were still slaves.

Moses wanted to help Israel, but he could do nothing. Besides, Israel did
not want his help. Pharaoh was angry with Moses for trying to help, so Moses ran
far away from Egypt to Midian in Arabia.

He was resting there by a well. Young women were trying to water their flocks.
When rough men stopped them, Moses helped the women. These were the daughters
of Jethro, priest of Midian. Moses was invited to stay in Jethro's house. He married
Jethro's daughter Zipporah and herded Jethro's flocks.

For forty years, Moses had lived in Egypt. There he was a wise and powerful
prince. Now he shepherded another man's sheep. He lived on the far side of
the desert. "I'm a stranger living in a strange land," Moses said.

Meanwhile, Israel cried and groaned in slavery. God heard them. He
remembered His promises to Abraham, Isaac, and Jacob. God saw
Israel in Egypt and understood their troubles.

Be a Protector

One day after Moses had grown up, he went out to his brothers
and saw how hard they worked. He saw an Egyptian
beating a Hebrew, one of his people.
EXODUS 2:11

M oses saw someone hurting one of his friends and he got mad! Can you blame him? Has anyone ever tried to hurt one of your brothers or sisters, or someone you love? It's hard to forgive a person who hurts someone you love. When we see a meanie picking on someone else, God wants us to tell a grown-up. You won't be a tattletale if you let your mom or dad know what's going on. Be brave. Speak up!

Lord, I don't want to be a tattletale, but I do want to protect other
kids from bullies. Give me courage to speak up, please! Amen.

God Appears in a Burning Bush

EXODUS 3:1–6

Moses had his flock on Mount Horeb. There, God appeared to him as a flame of fire in a bush. Moses saw the bush burning but not burned up. Moses wondered why the bush didn't burn up.

God called from the bush, "Moses, Moses."

"I'm here," Moses answered.

"Come no closer," God warned. "Take off your sandals. You're standing on holy ground. I am your ancestor's God—the God of Abraham, of Isaac, and of Jacob."

Moses hid his face and couldn't look at God.

God Still Speaks

The Lord saw him step aside to look. And God called to him from inside the bush, saying, "Moses, Moses!" Moses answered, "Here I am." God said, "Do not come near. Take your shoes off your feet. For the place where you are standing is holy ground."
Exodus 3:4–5

Can you imagine seeing God face-to-face? When God spoke to Moses from the burning bush, he must have been very surprised! Did you know that God still speaks to people today? Sometimes He whispers things to your heart. Other times He speaks through His Word, the Bible. Sometimes He uses people like your mom or dad to say, "I love you," or "You're doing great, kid!" Keep your eyes and ears open. Today God wants to tell you how much He adores you.

I'm listening for Your voice, Lord. And by the way, I love You, too!

Israel's Exodus

Exodus 12:30–14:14

Pharaoh called Moses and said, "Take Israel and get away from my people. Take everything you have and be gone."

Israel had lived in Egypt 430 years. Six hundred thousand men began the exodus that night. Of course, they had their wives and children with them. Their flocks and herds followed. They didn't forget to bring Joseph's coffin. When they came to Canaan, they buried Joseph as promised.

God was their leader. Israel could see the Lord ahead of them. In the daytime, there was a great cloud like a pillar. At night, they saw a pillar of fire. So they said, "The God of heaven and earth goes before us."

This great nation traveled southeast to the sea. They followed God in the pillar of cloud and of fire. But Pharaoh was sorry he'd let them go. Who would be his slaves? He led his army after them.

Israel faced the Red Sea. Mountains were on each side. Pharaoh and his army were close behind. Then Moses said, "Stand still and see how God will save you."

God Is a Good Guide

The Lord went before them, in a pillar of cloud during the day to lead them on the way, and in a pillar of fire during the night to give them light. So they could travel day and night.
EXODUS 13:21

Have you ever been on a trip? Moses took the Israelites (a lot of people) on a trip with him. It's hard to travel in a big group, but God told Moses He would take care of the details—like feeding and protecting them. He guided them with a cloud during the daytime and a pillar of fire at night. God still likes to guide His people, to show them which way to go. It's true! Ask your mom or dad about a time when God guided them someplace special.

Thanks for guiding me, Lord. When I don't know which way to go, You will always show me. Amen.

Escape through the Sea

Exodus 14:15–30

Trapped between the army and the Red Sea, Israel cried out. Moses said, "The Lord will fight for you," and lifted his staff over the sea. "You'll never see the Egyptians again."

All night an east wind blew. The water split in two and the sea became dry. Israel went into the sea on dry ground following the Lord. The water formed two walls.

The Egyptians chased after them. But the wheels fell from their chariots, and they tried to run. Just then, Moses lifted his staff again. The sea returned and Egypt drowned.

God Still Does Miracles

Then Moses put out his hand over the sea. And the Lord moved the
sea all night by a strong east wind. So the waters were divided.
EXODUS **14:21**

D o you know what a miracle is? It's when God does something that
we could *never* do on our own. In this story, God parted the sea
so that Moses and the Israelites could walk through. A big wind blew
back the waters and made a dry path through the sea. Moses and his
friends were protected from their enemies. What an amazing miracle!
God still does miracles today. Ask your mom or dad about a time when
God performed a miracle, when He took care of them in a special way.

Wow, God! You still do miracles today. That's amazing.
Thank You for the times You have protected
and cared for my family. Amen.

Moses, God, and the Mountain

Exodus 19:1–24:18

The nation of Israel traveled for three months. They finally arrived at Mount Sinai. This great mountain rises straight up from the desert. It is near the place where Moses saw the burning bush. Here, in front of the mountain, Israel camped.

God spoke to Moses from the mountain. "Don't let the people touch this mountain. It is a holy place. Soon, they will all see Me come to the mountaintop."

Three days later all Israel came to the mountain to meet God. Sinai was wrapped in smoke. God had come down on it in fire. The whole mountain shook wildly, and the people were terrified. A trumpet began to blast louder and louder. Moses spoke to God, and God answered in thunder. The people thought they would die. "Don't let God speak to us anymore," they begged.

Moses entered the cloud and thick darkness on the mountain. God called him to the mountaintop. He and God spoke together there for forty days. God told him about all the laws Israel should obey. God gave Moses two tablets made of stone. On these tablets God Himself had written the Ten Commandments.

Love Is the Best Rule

*Moses came and told the people all the Lord said and all the
Laws. All the people answered with one voice, saying,
"We will do all that the Lord has spoken."*
EXODUS 24:3

Moses went up on the mountain and God chatted with him, then gave him a list of ten rules to follow. We call these the Ten Commandments. Maybe you could ask your mom or dad to read the list to you. When you do, you will see that God wants us to love Him and love one another. Those are the two most important things. Have you ever been given a list of rules? *Clean your room. Obey your parents. Treat your brother or sister with love.* These rules are important, but remember, love is the very best rule!

*God, I want to make Your heart happy. I love You,
and I will love others. Amen.*

The Dazzling Face of Moses

Exodus 34:5–35:1

For the second time, Moses spent forty days with God. The Lord wrote His laws on the new tablets and talked with Moses.

Moses brought the tablets down the mountain. He didn't know that his face shone with God's light. His face was so dazzling that the people couldn't look at him.

Moses spoke to Israel about God's laws. He had to cover his face with a veil. The light hurt the eyes of the people when they saw him.

Spend Time in God's Presence

Moses came down from Mount Sinai with the two stone writings in his hand. He did not know that the skin of his face was shining because of his speaking with the Lord.
EXODUS 34:29

Sparkle, sparkle, shine! After he'd spent time in God's presence, Moses' face glowed! It was so bright that the people could hardly stand to look at him because it hurt their eyes. Did you know that you can spend time in God's presence, too? Every time you read your Bible and pray, you come into His presence. And when you leave, you have the shine of Jesus in your eyes. Others notice and wonder what you've been up to. You can say, "I've been spending time with Jesus!"

Lord, I love to spend time with You. Thanks for hanging out with me. I want to shine for You! Amen.

The Tabernacle of God

Exodus 35:1–40:38

On the mountain, God told Moses His plan for Israel. He showed Moses the way to build a special kind of tent. In it the people would meet with God. This tent was called the tabernacle. They also called it the tent of meeting.

Moses called for an offering to the Lord. Everyone brought gold and cloth, fine leather, oil and spices, beautiful wood, and precious stones. All this was used in building the tabernacle. Many people were skilled carpenters and handy with their hands. They came to help build the tent of meeting.

This was an expensive, large, and beautiful tent. It was made of the best materials exactly like the Lord planned it. Its walls were boards covered with gold. Over these the tent was hung. It was blue, scarlet, and purple linen cloth. This was covered with skins and hides.

Outside the tabernacle was a brass altar for offerings. There were beautiful pieces of special furniture inside. The entire tabernacle could be packed and carried on Israel's travels.

Finally, Moses and the people finished the tabernacle. The cloud that led them out of Egypt covered the tent. God's glory filled the tabernacle.

Meet with God

Then the cloud covered the meeting tent.
The shining-greatness of the Lord filled the holy tent.
EXODUS **40:34**

G od wanted a special place to meet with the people. That's why He asked them to build a beautiful tent with amazing things inside. He showed up in a big way! In fact, His shining brightness was so strong that Moses couldn't even go inside! Did you know that God loves to meet with His kids today, too? He wants you to have a special place where you can go to pray. Maybe it's your bedroom. Maybe it's in the living room. It could even be in a playhouse or a tent! Go to your very own special place and pray. God will be waiting for you!

Lord, thank You for meeting me in my special place.
Please don't ever let me forget to meet with You! Amen.

The Long Desert Journey

NUMBERS 14:1-45

The people of Israel were complaining. "We should have died in Egypt or the desert. Why does God want us to die in a war in Canaan? Let's all go back to Egypt." Suddenly the glory of God flashed and shone from the tabernacle.

God spoke: "How long will this people disobey and despise Me? They shall not enter Canaan. Instead they will all die in the desert. Their children will grow up, and only they will enter this good land. Tomorrow you must go back to the desert. You will wander there for forty years."

Then the people changed their minds. "No," they all said. "We'll not go back to the desert. We'll go straight into the land right now."

"You must not go into Canaan," Moses said. "God will not go with you." But they rushed to enter Canaan anyway. The tribes who lived there, the Canaanites and the Amalekites, attacked them. Many Israelites were killed. So they finally turned back into the desert.

For forty years, they moved through the desert. The old men died, and the young men were trained as warriors. Then they came back to Kadesh near Canaan where they began.

Happy Obedience

The Lord said to Moses, "How long will this people turn away from Me? How long will they not believe in Me, even after all the great works I have done among them?"
NUMBERS 14:11

Whoopsie-daisy! Some people *really* don't like to obey. They get one chance. Then two. Then three. But they still refuse to do the right thing. What about you? Has your mom ever said, "I'm counting to three!"? Your parents probably give you lots of chances to behave, but it's always better if you do it right away, without any chances at all. Obedience is a great way to show someone that you love them. So obey God and obey your parents, grandparents, and teachers. You will make everyone happy.

Lord, I don't want to have to ask for second chances.
I want to do the right thing, but I need Your help. Amen.

The Suffering of Job

Job 1:1–2:8

A man named Job lived east of Canaan. He was very rich and also very good. Once the angels were standing in front of God. Satan was there with them.

"Have you seen my servant Job?" God asked. "There's no one like him. He's blameless and right and rejects evil."

"Take away all he has. He'll curse You," Satan said.

"All right, Satan," God said. "Do what you want with him."

Soon trouble came to Job. His animals were driven away or killed with Job's shepherds. Then all his sons and daughters were killed. Their house fell in on them. All this happened in one day.

Job said, "I came into this world with nothing. I'll leave with nothing, too. The Lord gave me everything; He can take it away. The Lord's name is blessed."

God again said to Satan, "Have you seen Job? He's blameless and right."

"Give me power to make him sick. Then we'll see how good he is."

"All right, Satan," God said, "just don't kill him."

No Matter What

The Lord said to Satan, "Have you thought about My servant Job?
For there is no one like him on the earth. He is without blame,
a man who is right and good. He fears God and turns away from
sin. He still holds to his good ways, even when I allowed you
to go against him, and to destroy him for no reason."
JOB 2:3

Sometimes bad things happen to good people. It doesn't mean that God doesn't love them. Sometimes good people get sick, or they lose their jobs, or people say mean things about them. It doesn't seem fair. The best thing you can do when something bad happens is to go on loving God anyway. Good times or bad, happy or sad, He wants to know that you will love and serve Him.

Lord, I will go on loving You no matter what! Amen.

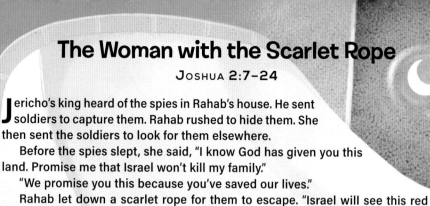

The Woman with the Scarlet Rope

JOSHUA 2:7–24

Jericho's king heard of the spies in Rahab's house. He sent soldiers to capture them. Rahab rushed to hide them. She then sent the soldiers to look for them elsewhere.

Before the spies slept, she said, "I know God has given you this land. Promise me that Israel won't kill my family."

"We promise you this because you've saved our lives."

Rahab let down a scarlet rope for them to escape. "Israel will see this red rope hanging out your window," they said. "It will be a sign for them not to harm you."

God Can Use Anyone

Then she let them down by a rope through the window.
She lived in her house that was built on top of the city wall.
JOSHUA 2:15

Some people think that God only chooses really important people to do great things, but that's not true. God can use anyone who has a willing heart, just like the woman, Rahab, in today's story. Whether you're rich or poor, young or old, He can use you. He's just looking for people with willing hearts. What about you? Do you want God to do great things through you? If so, just say, "Lord, here I am! Use me!"

I want to be used by You, God, to do great and mighty things.
I'm just a kid right now, but I know You can use me,
so I want to say, "Here I am!" Amen.

The Wall of Jericho Falls

JOSHUA 6:1–27

God said to Joshua, "I've given you the city of Jericho." He then told Joshua how to defeat the city. It was done God's way.

Israel's army went to the city as if to fight. With them went priests holding trumpets made of rams' horns. The ark of the covenant was carried along as they marched. For six days, while the trumpets blew, they marched around the city once. On the seventh day, they circled the city seven times. When Joshua ordered, Israel shouted! Then Jericho's wall fell down flat, and they took the city.

Trust God

"When you hear the long sound of the ram's horn, all the people should call out with a loud noise. The wall of the city will fall to the ground. And then all the people will all go in the city."
JOSHUA 6:5

Sometimes things look impossible. But remember, no matter *what* you're going through, miracles can still happen. You just have to have faith like Joshua did. Then you can look at impossible things and watch God do something supernatural. Have you ever seen a miracle? Did you ever watch a sick person get well or a mean person become kind? God still works lots of miracles today. They are all around you, so keep your eyes wide open.

I get it, Lord! You're still working miracles today, just like You did for Joshua when the wall fell down around Jericho! Amen.

Deborah Judges Israel

JUDGES 4:1-7

One of Israel's judges was Deborah. She was the only woman ever to judge Israel. People would come to see her in the hills of Ephraim. Deborah sat under a palm tree giving advice and solving problems. Like the other judges, Deborah had God's Spirit with her. This is why people followed her advice.

But in the north, a Canaanite king named Jabin attacked Israel. Israel had left God and was worshiping idols. Deborah sent for Barak. "The God of Israel commands you to raise an army. He'll let you defeat Jabin's army."

Great Women of God

Now Lappidoth's wife Deborah, a woman who spoke for God,
was judging Israel at that time.
JUDGES **4:4**

Deborah was an amazing woman! She listened for God's voice, then told others what He said. What an honor! Some people might say, "Why did God choose a woman to do this? Why didn't He pick a man?" God uses all sorts of people to share His Word with others. Are there any women in your life who tell you great things about God? Maybe your mom, your grandmother, or a teacher? Listen closely! You can learn a lot from these awesome ladies. And remember, God wants to use you, too!

God, thanks for speaking. I want to be like Deborah,
always listening for Your voice. Amen.

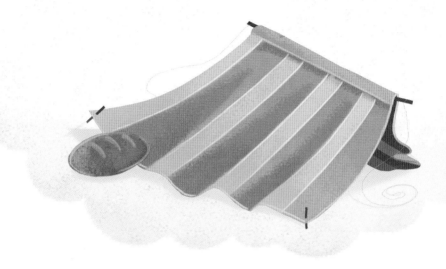

Gideon's Tiny Army

JUDGES 7:2–15

The Lord told Gideon, "Your army is too large. People will say, 'We won the victory by our own power.' Send home those who are afraid." Twenty-two thousand went away. Ten thousand stayed to fight.

Then the Lord said, "There are still too many troops. Take them to drink at the spring. Some will lap the water with their tongues. Others will kneel and scoop water with their hands."

Three hundred men lapped up the water. The rest scooped the water. "I'll use the three hundred that lapped to defeat Midian," God said. "The others may leave."

That night God told him, "Go to the enemy camp. You'll hear what they're saying. This will help you in the fight."

At Midian's enormous camp, Gideon heard a soldier tell another his dream. "I dreamed a loaf of bread tumbled into our camp. It hit the tent and knocked it down." Then the other said, "This is the sword of Gideon. God has given us all to him."

Gideon was glad to hear that Midian was afraid. He thanked God, returned to camp, and prepared for battle.

God Is on My Team

Then the Lord said to Gideon, "There are still too many people.
Bring them down to the water. I will test them for you there.
Whoever I say is to go with you will go. But whoever
I say is not to go with you will not go."
JUDGES 7:4

Gideon's army was very small. He didn't have a lot of people on his side. He probably wondered how he could win the battle, since the other team had more people on it. But guess what? When God is on your side, it doesn't matter how many people you have on your team. Even if it's just you and God, that's enough to win the battle. Have you figured out yet that God is very powerful? It's true! He can do great things.

Lord, I've got You on my team and that's enough!
Thanks for sticking with me! Amen.

The Strongman Samson

JUDGES 13:2–16:15

A child was born named Samson. He became the strongest man mentioned in the Bible. He didn't lead an army in war like Gideon. The things he did to set his people free, he did alone.

Samson met a Philistine woman in Timnah. "I want her for my wife," he told his father. This didn't make Samson's parents happy. But they didn't know God would use this marriage. It would help free Israel from the Philistines.

Three times Delilah begged Samson, "Tell me the secret of your strength."

"Tie me with fresh bowstrings," Samson said. But he broke them like burning string.

"Tie me with new ropes. Then I'll lose my strength." But he broke these ropes like thread.

"Weave my hair into your loom like cloth. Then I'll be like everyone else." While Samson slept, Delilah wove. But when the Philistines tried to capture him, Samson broke the loom.

"How can you tell me you love me?" Delilah cried. "You've lied to me."

Strong in the Lord

The leaders of the Philistines came to [Delilah], saying,
"Tempt Samson to tell you the secret of his powerful strength.
Find out how we can get power over him so we can tie him and
hold him. Then we will each give you 1,100 pieces of silver."
JUDGES 16:5

S amson was a superstrong man! If you tied ropes around his arms, he could break through those ropes like they were pieces of thread. Wow! What about you? Are you strong? The Bible says you will grow strong in the Lord if you pray and study His Word. That doesn't mean you'll have big muscles like Samson, but it does mean that your spirit will be strong. You will become a mighty child of God!

I want to be strong like Samson, Lord. I will pray and study the
Bible so that my spiritual muscles will grow! Amen.

Samson's Strength Is Lost

JUDGES 16:16-22

Samson was tired of Delilah's pleading and nagging. Day after day, she begged him for the secret of his strength. So he finally told her the mystery. "My hair has never been cut," he said. "I've been a Nazirite priest for God since my birth. If my hair was cut, my Nazirite vow would be broken. God would leave me and so would my great strength."

Delilah smiled. At last she had the secret. The Philistine chiefs came with money in their hands. That night Samson slept with his head in Delilah's lap. He was sound asleep. The Philistines quietly cut off Samson's long hair. He began to weaken and all his strength left. Then Delilah shouted, "Wake up, Samson! The Philistines are after you!"

Samson jumped up, thinking, *This is like the other times. I'll shake them off.* He didn't know that the Lord had left him. His hair was cut and his vow was broken. The Philistines easily took Samson prisoner and gouged out his eyes.

They took him down to Gaza. Locked in bronze shackles, Samson turned the grindstone in their mill. But slowly his hair began to grow long again.

Strong Inside and Out

So he told her all that was in his mind. He said to her, "My hair has never been cut. For I have been a Nazirite to God from the time I was born. If my hair is cut, my strength will leave me. I will become weak and be like any other man."
JUDGES 16:17

The secret to Samson's strength was in his hair. Delilah knew that, so she had the bad guys cut off his hair while he was sleeping. What a meanie! What about you? Where does your strength come from? Some people would say, "From my muscles!" But you know the truth. Your strength comes from the Lord. And it's not enough to be strong on the outside; you have to be strong on the inside, too. After all, a strong person is a person who makes good decisions.

Thanks for making me superstrong, Lord! Amen.

Ruth Joins Naomi

RUTH 1:1-22

A famine came to the land when the judges ruled Israel. Elimelech of Bethlehem moved his family to Moab. After ten years there, Elimelech died. His two sons were married to women of Moab. But then they died, too. So Elimelech's wife, Naomi, and her daughters-in-law were widows.

Naomi heard that God had brought good harvests to Israel. She decided to return. She told each of her sons' wives, "Return to your mother's home. May God be kind to you and give you a new husband." She kissed them both, and they wept together.

One young widow, Orpah, did go back to her family. But the second, Ruth, wouldn't leave Naomi. "See," said Naomi, "Orpah has returned to her people and her gods. You go, too."

"Don't make me leave you or stop following you," Ruth said. "Where you go, I'll go. Where you live, I'll live. Your people will be my people, and your God, my God. Where you die, I'll die, and there I'll be buried. Only death will come between us."

Naomi saw that Ruth was firm. She said no more, and they returned together to Bethlehem.

Stick Like Glue

But Ruth said, "Do not beg me to leave you or turn away from following you. I will go where you go. I will live where you live. Your people will be my people. And your God will be my God."
RUTH 1:16

Have you ever had a friend you loved a lot? Those people are called BFFs (best friends forever). That's how it was with Ruth and Naomi. Ruth wanted to stick like glue to Naomi because she loved her so deeply. God wants you to have special stick-like-glue friends, too! They make life so much fun. Who do you love to be with? Your mom? Your dad? Your brothers and sisters? Your grandparents? A friend from school? Choose the ones you love and stick to them in good times and in bad.

Thanks for my special friends, Lord!
I want to stick with them forever. Amen.

Ruth Meets Boaz

RUTH 2:1–9

The time of barley harvest had come to Bethlehem. When they harvested their fields, the Israelites always left some grain standing. This grain was left for the poor to be gleaned, or gathered, later.

Ruth went out to glean in the fields of a man named Boaz. He was of the family of Elimelech, Naomi's dead husband. Boaz was watching the harvest and saw Ruth. "Who is the young woman gleaning in the field?" he asked the workers.

"She came back with Naomi from Moab," they answered. Boaz gave Ruth water and urged her to stay in his field.

Stay in His Field

Then Boaz said to Ruth, "Be careful to listen, my daughter. Do not go to gather grain in another field. Do not leave this one. But stay here with my women who gather grain."
RUTH 2:8

Naomi told Ruth to stay in the field of a man named Boaz and to follow his instructions. Naomi knew that Ruth would be safe there. That's how it is with you and God. You're His child, and He plans to take good care of you, to keep you safe. He wants you to stay in His field, to follow His rules, to enjoy His love. When you stick with Jesus, you will have a wonderfully satisfying life. So stay in His field and grow big and strong!

Lord, I will stay in Your field! I won't go wandering off. I'll love You forever, Jesus! Amen.

Samuel Stays in God's House

1 SAMUEL 1:1–2:25

There was once a priest and judge of Israel named Eli. He and his sons served God in the tabernacle at Shiloh. Every year a man named Elkanah and his family worshiped there. Like many men in those days, Elkanah had two wives. One had children. The other, named Hannah, did not. Hannah often cried because she couldn't have children.

One year at Shiloh, Eli saw Hannah praying outside the tabernacle. "O Lord," she said, "look how sad I am. Remember me and allow me to have a little boy. I will give him to You as a Nazirite priest."

The Lord heard Hannah's prayer and gave her a baby boy. She named him Samuel, which means "asked of God." When Samuel was still a little child, she brought him to Eli. Hannah said to the priest, "I asked God for this boy. I promised him to the Lord for all his life. Let him stay here with you and grow up in God's house."

So little Samuel stayed in Shiloh, helping Eli, the old priest. Eli's own sons were priests, but they were also scoundrels. So Samuel was a comfort to Eli.

Don't Give Up

Then she made a promise and said, "O Lord of All, be sure to look on the trouble of Your woman servant, and remember me. Do not forget Your woman servant, but give me a son. If You will, then I will give him to the Lord all his life. And no hair will ever be cut from his head."
1 SAMUEL 1:11

Hannah prayed for a *really* long time because she wanted to have a baby. She begged God for a baby boy, and—after many prayers—God gave her what she asked for. Samuel was born, and Hannah dedicated him to the Lord. Maybe you've been praying for something for a long time. Maybe it seems like God isn't listening or doesn't care. God always listens and always cares! So don't give up. Keep praying like Hannah.

Lord, I won't give up. I know You're listening to my prayers and You care about my needs. Amen.

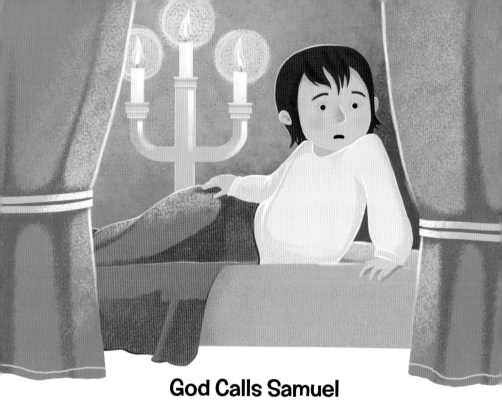

God Calls Samuel

1 SAMUEL 3:1–10

One night, Samuel lay resting in the tabernacle. The Lord called to him, "Samuel, Samuel."

"Here I am!" said Samuel, and he ran to Eli's room. "Did you call me?"

"No," Eli answered. "Go back to bed, my son."

The same thing happened a second time. Samuel didn't know God then, or God's words.

Then Samuel was called a third time. At last, Eli understood that the Lord was calling the boy. Eli then told Samuel how to answer.

The Lord came and stood there calling as before. Samuel answered, "Speak, Lord, for Your servant is listening."

Listen for God's Voice

*The Lord called Samuel again for the third time. He got up
and went to Eli, and said, "Here I am, for you called me."
Then Eli understood that the Lord was calling the boy.*
1 Samuel 3:8

Shh! Can you hear it? Samuel was just a little boy when God spoke
to him for the first time. He was sound asleep when God said,
"Samuel! Samuel!" Samuel got out of bed and went to Eli, the priest,
because he thought Eli was talking to him. But it wasn't Eli. . .it was
God! Did you know that God still speaks today? Sometimes if you're
really still and quiet, you can hear Him whisper things like, "I love you!"
or "Great job!" He also speaks through His Word, the Bible. What an
amazing God we serve!

I'm listening, Lord! What do You have to say to me today? Amen.

God Chooses Israel's King

1 Samuel 9:1-25

Saul, a wealthy Benjamite, was a tall, handsome young man. Saul and a servant were near Zuph searching for stray donkeys. The servant said, "A prophet lives in this town. He may know where the donkeys are."

The day before, the Lord had spoken to Samuel. "Tomorrow, a man will come from Benjamin. Make him the king of Israel. He'll save My people from the Philistines." When Samuel saw Saul walking up the hill, God spoke again. "This is the man I told you about yesterday."

Saul asked Samuel, "Where does the prophet live?"

"I'm the prophet," Samuel replied. "Come with me, and we'll eat together. And don't worry about the donkeys. They've been found. Do you know that Israel hopes in you and your father's house?"

"I'm from Benjamin," Saul replied. "That's the smallest tribe in Israel. My family is the smallest in Benjamin. Why do you talk to me like this?"

But Samuel brought Saul to the feast. He was given the best seat. His food was the finest of all that was served.

Special Jobs

When Samuel saw Saul, the Lord said to him, "Here is the man I told you about. He is the one who will rule over My people."
1 SAMUEL 9:17

Did you know that God has special jobs for special people? It was true for King Saul, and it's true for the people you know, too. Your mom? She has a special job. So does your dad, your brothers and sisters, your teachers, your grandparents, and so on. Everyone who loves the Lord has a special job to do. When you get older, you can ask God about your special job. He has a lot of great things ahead for you, so get ready—you're really going places!

Lord, I am so glad You have special jobs for all of us. I can't wait to find out what I'm going to be when I grow up! Amen.

David—the Anointed Boy

1 Samuel 16:1–12

God spoke to Samuel again: "Bring oil to Bethlehem. There you'll anoint Jesse's son as the new king."

At Bethlehem, Samuel offered God a sacrifice. Jesse and his seven sons were there. Samuel thought, *I'll anoint one of these young men.* But God said, "They are good-looking, but I don't want them. People only see what others look like. But I look at their heart."

"Do you have another son?" asked Samuel.

"My youngest son, David, is with the sheep."

Jesse sent for David. When the boy arrived, God said, "Anoint him. This is the one."

God Looks at the Heart

*But the Lord said to Samuel, "Do not look at the way he looks
on the outside or how tall he is, because I have not chosen him.
For the Lord does not look at the things man looks at. A man looks
at the outside of a person, but the Lord looks at the heart."*
1 SAMUEL 16:7

If you watch many movies, you've probably noticed that every movie princess is pretty and every prince is handsome. Some people think that the pretty (or supersmart) people are more special than others, but that's not true. God doesn't judge us by how we look or by our talents. He loves us all equally. Remember, God is looking at your heart, nothing else. Keep it looking good!

*Thanks for showing me that I shouldn't judge people by how
they look, Lord. I'll do my best to look at their hearts! Amen.*

David—the Musician-King

1 Samuel 16:13-23

David was only about fifteen, with bright eyes and rosy cheeks. Samuel anointed him with oil as his older brothers watched. God's Spirit was with David from that day on. At the same time, Saul became very gloomy. He was not at peace with God.

Because David played the harp well, Jesse sent him to Saul. Saul's servants thought that the music would help cheer the king. Saul loved David. His music made the king feel better. But Saul didn't know that Samuel had anointed David. The boy who played the harp for Saul was Israel's future king.

A Special Gift

When the bad spirit sent from God came upon Saul, David would take the harp and play it with his hand. And Saul would receive new strength and be well. The bad spirit would leave him.
1 SAMUEL 16:23

David had a special talent, one that was given to him by God. He knew how to play the harp. When David played his harp, something amazing happened. King Saul would calm down and feel better. Some people probably thought it was because David was extra talented, but really it happened because God chose David for this special gift. God still anoints people today, just like He did in Bible times.

Thanks for giving Your kids special gifts, Lord! Amen.

David—the Shepherd-Warrior

1 Samuel 17:1-45

While Saul was king, the Philistines battled with Israel. There was a giant Philistine named Goliath. He was nine feet tall and impossible to fight. He dared any Israelite to fight him. "Let him kill me!" Goliath roared. "Then we'll be your servants." But Saul's army was afraid.

"Who's this?" David asked. "Don't let him defy God's army." With his shepherd's staff in hand, David went to fight Goliath. From a stream, David picked five stones for his slingshot.

David challenged Goliath: "You come with a sword. I come in the name of the Lord of Hosts."

God Is on Your Side

"Your servant has killed both the lion and the bear. And this Philistine who has not gone through our religious act will be like one of them. For he has made fun of the armies of the living God."
1 SAMUEL 17:36

Wowza, talk about tall! When David the shepherd boy faced the mighty giant Goliath, he wasn't afraid. He knew that God was on his side. When you know that God is on your side, there's no reason to be frightened. Did you know that God is on your side? No matter what you go through, no matter how many giants you face, you will never ever have to be afraid, because the Lord is with you. You're a winner as long as you stick with Him!

I'm so glad I'm Your kid, Lord! Thanks for being on my side. Amen.

David—the Giant Killer

1 Samuel 17:46–52

Goliath saw David carrying a shepherd's staff. "You're here to fight me with a stick?" Goliath cursed. "Do you think I'm a dog?"

"Today, God will give me your life!" David shouted. "I'll strike you down and cut off your head. The birds and animals will feast on the Philistine army. The earth will know there's a God in Israel."

Then, running at Goliath, David put a stone in his slingshot. He hurled the stone deep into the giant's forehead. Goliath fell dead to the ground. That day, David won a great victory for Israel.

A Big Victory!

David put his hand into his bag, took out a stone and threw it, and hit the Philistine on his forehead. The stone went into his forehead, so that he fell on his face to the ground.
1 SAMUEL 17:49

David faced a mighty giant who was threatening his people. This guy was big. . .and mean! (Have you ever known any meanies like this? What bullies!) Here's the good news: David won the battle with just one little stone. Sometimes in your life you will have to face giants, but God will give you the victory, just like He did for David, as long as you remember that He's the One doing the fighting. Who do you trust today?

God, I put my trust in You. I won't trust in my own strength or in anyone else. Thanks for giving me the victory, Lord! Amen.

David—the Joyful Dancer

2 Samuel 6:1-23

The ark of the covenant had been hidden away while Saul ruled. David decided it was time to bring it to Jerusalem. A new oxcart was built just to carry the ark. As it rolled toward Jerusalem, David and other Israelites followed behind. They sang and made music and danced with all their strength.

The tabernacle was set up on Mount Zion. The priests carried the ark into the tent of meeting, and offerings were burned to the Lord. Israel was shouting with joy, and David used all his strength dancing before the Lord.

Dancing before the Lord

As the special box of the Lord came into the city of David,
Saul's daughter Michal looked out of the window. She saw
King David jumping and dancing before the Lord,
and she hated him in her heart.
2 SAMUEL 6:16

Wiggle those toes! Clap those hands! David got so excited when the ark of the covenant came back to Jerusalem that he did a happy dance! He just couldn't help himself. He sang and danced with all his might. Have you ever done a happy dance? It's a fun way to worship God. The next time you're excited, why not move your hands and feet? Go ahead! God loves when His kids dance before Him. What a wonderful way to worship the King of kings!

I love to dance before You, Lord!
What a fun way to praise You. Amen.

Solomon Prays for Wisdom

1 Kings 3:3-28

One night the Lord came to Solomon in a dream. "What would you like Me to give you?" God asked.

Solomon said, "I am only a young man, Lord. I don't know how to rule this great people. Give me wisdom and knowledge to know right and wrong."

The Lord was pleased that Solomon had asked this. "You didn't ask for a long life," God said. "Nor did you ask for riches, victory, or power. Instead you've asked for wisdom to judge My people. So I give you greater wisdom than any other king. No other ruler will ever have more wisdom than you. And because you've asked only for this, I'll give you more. You'll have riches and honor. No other ruler will compare to you. Obey My words like your father, David, obeyed. Then you'll have a long life and rule for many years."

Solomon could build God's great temple. He could also wisely judge small matters.

Wisdom Comes from God

And the king said, "Divide the living child in two.
Give half to the one woman and half to the other."
1 Kings 3:25

A lot of kids are super-duper smart. They study and learn their lessons in school. They get an A+ on every test. Some are even teacher's pet. But there's a difference between being smart and having godly wisdom. Even smart people act unwise at times. God wants you to have His special wisdom. You can't learn it from a book or study it in school. It's a special gift that comes straight from God. Today, why not ask God to make you wise?

Lord, please make me wise! I want to have Your special godly
wisdom so I can make good decisions like Solomon. Amen.

God's Temple Is Built

1 Kings 5:1–8:66

The most important thing Solomon did was build God's temple. It stood on Mount Moriah in Jerusalem.

The stones of the temple walls were cut to fit perfectly. The cedar posts and beams were carved and then brought to Jerusalem. So while the temple was built there was very little noise. It was designed like the tabernacle, only much larger. Also the temple was not a tent. It was strongly built of stone and cedarwood.

In seven years, the temple was complete. The ark was placed in the holy of holies. Solomon and the people worshiped there.

A Special Project

"So I plan to build a house for the name of the Lord my God. Because the Lord said to my father David, 'I will set your son on your throne in your place. He will build the house for My name.'"
1 KINGS 5:5

God gave Solomon a special project. He told him to build a temple on Mount Moriah in Jerusalem. Solomon did what he was told, and he did it lickety-split! He built the temple in seven years' time. God loves to give His kids special projects like this. You never know what He's going to ask you to do. If the Lord asks you to do something special, will you be like Solomon and complete the task? If so, then the Lord will probably have even more projects for you!

I love when You give me projects to do, Lord.
I want to complete every one. Amen.

Elijah and the Widow of Zarephath

1 KINGS 17:8–18

Since Elijah had no water, God told him, "Go and live in Zarephath. I've told a widow there to feed you." So Elijah journeyed to Zarephath. He found the widow near the gate gathering firewood.

"Bring me a little water," he asked. As the widow went for water, Elijah called to her again. "Bring me a bit of bread as well."

The widow answered, "I am about to bake bread. Then all my flour and oil will be gone. My son and I will eat it, lie down, and die."

"First make bread for me," Elijah said. "The God of Israel says this: 'Your flour and oil will last until rain comes again.' " The widow believed him. The jar that held her flour was never empty. The jug of oil didn't run out. This happened exactly as Elijah had said it would.

Give What You Have

But she said, "As the Lord your God lives, I have no bread. I only have enough flour in the jar to fill a hand, and a little oil in the jar. See, I am gathering a few sticks so I may go in and make it ready for me and my son. Then we will eat it and die."
1 Kings 17:12

Grumble, grumble, growl, growl! That's what Elijah's tummy sounded like. The widowed woman gave up her flour and oil, but God multiplied them and gave them back to her. God still loves when His kids give what they have. He multiplies your gifts. Even if you only have a little bit of money to put in the offering basket, He loves that! Even if your talents and abilities seem small, give them anyway. God will always multiply whatever you give.

Today I give You what I have, Lord—my time, talents, and treasures. Amen.

Elijah Soars in a Whirlwind

2 Kings 2:11–12

"Tell me, Elisha. What can I do for you before I'm taken?" Elijah asked.

"Please give me a double share of your spirit," Elisha said.

"That is hard. But if you see me as I'm taken away, it's yours."

The two prophets continued walking and talking. Suddenly, a chariot of fire pulled by flaming horses divided them. Elijah soared in a whirlwind into heaven.

Elisha watched, crying out, "Father, Father! The chariots of Israel and its horsemen!" When Elijah was out of sight, Elisha tore his clothes in grief.

A Trip to Heaven

As they went on and talked, a war-wagon of fire and horses of fire came between them. And Elijah went up by a wind-storm to heaven.
2 Kings 2:11

Whoosh! What a windstorm! Elisha was sad when his friend Elijah went to heaven. Maybe you know what that feels like. When someone you know goes to heaven, you miss them a lot. But here's some good news: if you ask Jesus to live in your heart, you will get to go to heaven someday, too. You will see your friends again when you get there. Isn't that amazing! It's okay to miss them now, but one day you will be together again and live in heaven forever!

Thanks for heaven, Lord! I'm excited to get there.
What a wonderful trip it will be! Amen.

A Captain Becomes King

2 KINGS 9:1–13

"Take this oil," Elisha said to a young prophet. "Go to Ramoth-gilead. Find Jehu. Then say, 'The Lord says this: I've anointed you king over Israel.' When you're done, come back right away."

The young prophet took the flask of oil to Ramoth-gilead. He found the captains sitting together in Israel's camp. "I have a message for you, Commander," he said.

"For which one of us?" Jehu asked.

"The message is for you, sir."

The prophet poured the oil on Jehu's head. "The Lord says this: 'I've anointed you as king over my people Israel.' You'll destroy Ahab's family because they killed God's prophets." Then the prophet left.

"Why did that madman come to you?" the others asked Jehu.

"No reason. You know how they babble."

"Tell us the truth."

"I've just been anointed king over Israel."

The captains threw their robes in front of Jehu's feet. A trumpet blared, and they all shouted, "Jehu is king!"

Chosen to Be King

"Then take the jar of oil and pour it on his head and say, 'The Lord says, "I have chosen you to be the king of Israel." ' Then open the door and run. Do not wait."
2 KINGS 9:3

⚬

It might seem a little strange that the prophet Elisha would pour oil on Jehu's head, but this was how he made the announcement "Jehu will be king!" Sometimes God uses interesting ways to let people know things. How would you feel if God picked you to be a king or queen? What kind of ruler would you be? Chances are good that Jehu was surprised by the announcement. You would be, too! God has special things in mind for you. Maybe you won't be a king or queen, but great days are coming.

⚬

I'm excited to see the great things You have in store for me, Lord. Amen.

Elisha's Life-Giving Bones

2 Kings 13:14–25

Joash, Jehu's grandson, was Israel's king when Elisha was about to die. "My father, my father!" Joash wept. "You're more important than Israel's horses and chariots."

"Take a bow and arrows and draw back the bowstring," said Elisha.

Elisha put his hands on the king's hands. "Open the window and shoot." And Joash did so. "This is the Lord's arrow of victory over Syria."

"Now take the arrows and hit the ground with them." Joash hit the ground with the arrows three times. "Why did you stop? You should have hit the ground five or six times. Then you would have had that many victories. Now you'll beat Syria three times and no more."

Soon Elisha died and was buried in a cave. The next year a band of Moabites buried a man in the same place. When this man's body touched Elisha's bones, life returned to it and the Moabite stood up on his feet.

True to Elisha's word, Israel defeated Syria three times. Israel's captured cities were taken back from Syria's control.

New Life

*As a man was being buried, some Moabite soldiers were seen,
so the man was thrown into Elisha's grave. When the man touched
the bones of Elisha, he came alive and stood up on his feet.*
2 Kings 13:21

God likes to bring things back to life again. Sound impossible? It's not! Nothing is impossible with God. Here's an example: Sometimes people have dreams or wishes. After a while they forget about them. But then God brings them back to life. Suddenly the person is dreaming again, wishing again. What about you? Do you have any dreams or wishes? What are you hoping for? Ask God to breathe new life into your dreams, and then. . .hold on! Maybe He'll perform a miracle, like He did with Elisha's bones!

*Lord, I can't wait to see how You breathe new
life into my dreams. I'm so excited! Amen.*

Jonah Runs from the Creator

JONAH 1:1–11

Syria was losing power. But Assyria was rising up. Its capital city, Nineveh, was huge. A man would take three days to walk through it. Israel was in danger of falling under Assyria's power. At that time, the Lord spoke to Jonah. "Go to Nineveh. Cry out and speak to them. I know of their wickedness."

Jonah didn't want to do this. Instead, he went the other way, to the seaport at Joppa. There he sailed for Tarshish, still farther from Nineveh. But the Lord threw a great wind onto the sea. There was a mighty storm. The ship was in danger, and the crew each prayed to his god.

They lightened the ship's load by throwing cargo overboard. That's when they discovered Jonah sleeping in the hold. "How can you sleep at a time like this? Get up. Call on your God to save us."

"We must find the man who has caused our distress." So the sailors decided to draw straws. Jonah lost the draw.

"I'm running away from the God who created the sea and land," he told them. Then the sailors were even more afraid.

"No wonder this has happened." They trembled.

Go Where God Says

But Jonah ran away from the Lord going toward Tarshish.
He went down to Joppa and found a ship which was going
to Tarshish. Jonah paid money, and got on the ship
to go with them, to get away from the Lord.
JONAH 1:3

When God tells us where to go, we should listen and obey. Jonah was scared to go to Nineveh, so he ran away and went the opposite direction. Oops, not a good idea! Have you ever gone the wrong way? Maybe your mom told you to go clean your room, but you went into the kitchen instead and took a cookie from the cookie jar. You knew you should go the right way, but you didn't want to. We should always do what God (and Mom!) says.

Lord, I want to go Your way so I don't ever get lost! Amen.

A Fish Spits Out Jonah

Jonah 1:11–2:10

The waves were running high. The ship was in danger. "What shall we do to calm the sea?" the sailors asked.

"Throw me into the sea," Jonah answered. "I've caused this trouble." But the sailors tried to row to shore. Finally, they could do no more. Praying for forgiveness, they threw Jonah overboard. Immediately, the sea stopped raging.

The Lord sent a big fish to swallow Jonah. He was in its belly for three days and nights. Jonah prayed to God from within the fish. The Lord spoke to the fish. It spit Jonah onto the beach.

Trapped!

Then Jonah prayed to the Lord his God while in the stomach of the fish, saying, "I called out to the Lord because of my trouble, and He answered me. I cried for help from the place of the dead, and You heard my voice."
JONAH 2:1–2

Jonah disobeyed God and ended up in the belly of a large fish. Sometimes when we do the wrong thing, we end up trapped. Our bad choices can take us to places we don't want to go. Has that ever happened to you? Maybe you disobeyed and were put in time-out. It's no fun to be trapped by our sins. That's one reason why we always need to strive to do the right thing. Obedience takes us to happy places. Sin takes us to sad places.

I want to go to happy places, Lord,
so I'll keep following You. Amen.

God Calls Isaiah

ISAIAH 6:1–9

Ahaz was the son of a good king, Jotham, who believed in God. But he worshiped Baal and burned his sons as sacrifices. Ahaz made sacrifices—on hills, in valleys, and under every green tree.

When Edom attacked Judah, Ahaz asked Assyria for help. But instead of helping, they took over Judah. Ahaz was robbed of everything because of his sins. Judah was oppressed under Assyria.

God's prophet Isaiah lived in the days of these kings. Isaiah was worshiping in the temple when he saw God on His throne surrounded by angels. The temple shook with voices: "Holy, holy, holy is the Lord of hosts."

Isaiah trembled, saying, "I'm a man with unclean lips, yet I've seen the Lord God." Then an angel brought a coal from the altar. The burning coal touched Isaiah's lips.

"Your sin is taken away. You are made clean."

The Lord said, "Who will be My messenger to the people?"

"Here I am, Lord," Isaiah said. "Send me."

The Lord replied, "Go and speak to My people."

Send Me!

*In the year of King Uzziah's death, I saw the Lord sitting
on a throne, high and honored. His long clothing
spread out and filled the house of God.*
ISAIAH **6:1**

*H*ello! Is anyone listening? God is looking for people who will tell others about Him. Isaiah was one of those people. You are one of those people, too. It's true! God wants to use you to tell your friends about how great He is! What can you share with others? You could tell them about the time you were sick and God made you better. Share about the time your friend's dad lost his job and God found him another one. If you stop to think about it, there are many great God stories you could tell!

*Lord, I want to be Your messenger like Isaiah was.
I'll share Your stories! Amen.*

The Sundial Moves Backward

2 KINGS 20:1–21

The Assyrians had invaded Judah. Jerusalem was in danger. King Hezekiah became sick and was near death. Isaiah the prophet came to speak with him.

"The Lord says: 'Get your life prepared, because you will die. You'll not get better.' "

Hezekiah prayed: "Remember, O Lord, how I've been faithful to You. I've done what is good for You with my whole heart."

Isaiah was walking away from the palace. "Turn," God said, "and talk with Hezekiah again. Say, 'The God of your ancestor David says: I've heard your prayer and seen your tears. I'll heal you and add fifteen years to your life. The city will be saved from Assyria.' "

"How will the Lord prove that He will heal me?" Hezekiah asked Isaiah.

"You choose the sign," answered Isaiah. "Shall the sundial gain ten minutes or lose ten minutes?"

"It normally gains time. Let the shadow go backward."

Isaiah cried to God, and the shadow moved backward by ten minutes. In three days, Hezekiah was well.

Prayer Changes Things

So Isaiah the man of God cried to the Lord, and the Lord brought the shadow back ten steps, on the steps set up by King Ahaz.
2 KINGS 20:11

A man named Hezekiah was very ill. Everyone thought he would die. But Hezekiah wasn't ready to die, so he decided to pray. He begged God to heal him. Guess what? The Lord chose to heal Hezekiah and gave him many more years to live. Wow! Great things can happen when we pray! God is listening, and He cares. Now think of a time when God answered your prayer. What did you ask for? How did He answer? Aren't you glad we serve a God who cares about our prayers?

Father, thank You for caring about my prayers.
I'm so happy to know You're listening! Amen.

Jeremiah's Vision of the Figs

JEREMIAH 24:1–10

Jehoiakim's young son, Jehoiachin, was made Judah's king. But Nebuchadnezzar, Babylon's king, overran Jerusalem and Judah. He captured the king and other nobles and took them to Babylon.

After this, Jeremiah had a vision of the future. He saw two baskets of figs. "What do you see, Jeremiah?" the Lord asked.

"Figs. The good figs are very good. The bad ones are so bad they can't be eaten."

The Lord explained this. "The captives taken to Babylon are like the good figs. I'll care for them and bring them back to this land. They'll be My people and I'll be their God. The bad figs are like the people left in the land. These include their king, Zedekiah, his princes, and his people. They will suffer and be killed. Plagues and famine will come to them until they are no more."

So Jeremiah wrote to the captives in Babylon. "Build houses, plant gardens, and have children. Let them be married in that land when they grow. After seventy years, you'll return to your own land in peace. God's thoughts are of peace and kindness toward you."

Good and Bad

"This is what the Lord God of Israel says: 'Like these good figs, so will I think of the people of Judah as being good, whom I have sent away from this place into the land of the Babylonians.'"
JEREMIAH **24:5**

This world is filled with good and bad people. Sometimes it's hard to know which are which, because the bad ones can be sneaky. But God sees all the way to the heart of a person. He knows the good from the bad. He wants to protect you from bad people so that you can live a happy life. Stay far away from kids who are doing naughty things. Stick with the good ones, and things will go well for you.

Thanks for the reminder that there are good and bad people in this world, Lord. Help me to stick with the good ones. Amen.

The Valley of Dry Bones

EZEKIEL 37:1–28

T he Lord sent prophets to the Israelites even in Babylon. Ezekiel prophesied about Israel's future:

"The Lord's Spirit brought me to a valley. It was full of bones. There were many, many bones all around, and they were very dry. The Lord asked me, 'Man, can these bones live?'

" 'You know, Lord,' I answered.

" 'Then speak to them. Tell them the Lord says this: I'll make breath come into you and you'll live. I'll make muscles and skin to come onto you. I'll give you breath. Then you'll know that I'm the Lord.'

"So I spoke these things to the dry bones. Suddenly, there was a noise. I heard rattling, and the bones came together. Muscles and skin covered them. I spoke to the four winds and breath entered the bodies. They were alive, standing on their feet.

" 'This is the nation of Israel. Tell them that I'll bring you up from captivity. I'll bring you back to the land of Israel. I'll put My Spirit in you and you'll live. Then you'll know that your God has spoken and will act.' "

God Does New Things

"This is what the Lord God says to these bones:
'I will make breath come into you, and you will come to life.'"
EZEKIEL **37:5**

The nation of Israel was in a real mess. They were living like slaves. But their story wasn't over yet! Sometimes you think a story is over when the "once upon a time" is just getting started. God likes to give new beginnings. That's what He did for Israel, and that's what He'll do for you. Some people get sick and think they won't get well, but the Lord heals them. Some people lose their house and think they won't get another one, but God provides a new home. He's always giving second chances and new beginnings. That's the kind of God we serve.

Thanks for new beginnings, Lord.
My "once upon a time" is just getting started! Amen.

Daniel and His Friends

DANIEL 1:1–21

Among the captives in Babylon was a young man named Daniel. God prepared him to become a great prophet of Israel.

King Nebuchadnezzar wanted young Jews to serve in his palace. They were to be bright, handsome, strong young men. Each must learn the Babylonian language and read its books. Wise men would teach them for three years. Then they would have jobs in the royal palace.

Among them were Daniel, Hananiah, Mishael, and Azariah. These men were from Judah. The king ordered that they be given Babylonian names. They were then called Belteshazzar, Shadrach, Meshach, and Abednego.

Daniel and his friends came to Nebuchadnezzar's palace. But their food had been offered to idols. Daniel went to the palace master. "Please don't make me dishonor myself by eating food given to idols."

"The king himself has given you this food. If you don't eat it, you won't be healthy. Then my life could be in danger of the king's anger."

"Let's try it for ten days," Daniel suggested. "Just give us vegetables to eat and water to drink. Then see if we're healthy."

The palace master agreed. After ten days, Daniel and his three friends looked healthier than the others. So they never ate the idols' food. God gave these four wisdom and skill in Babylonian knowledge. Daniel also could understand dreams and visions.

After three years' training they were brought to Nebuchadnezzar. The king spoke with them. No one could compare with Daniel, Hananiah, Mishael, and Azariah. They became part of the king's own court. The king was pleased. These four were ten times better than his own magicians and psychics.

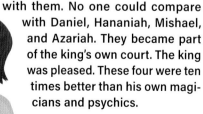

Healthy and Strong

"Test your servants for ten days. Give us only vegetables to eat and water to drink. Then compare how we look with the young men who are eating the king's best food. And do with us what you think is best by what you see."
DANIEL 1:12–13

B ad people are always tempting good people to do the wrong things. They say things like, "You won't get in trouble," or "Who cares if it's wrong? Let's do it anyway." You're not falling for that, though! You're like Daniel. He knew right from wrong, and he chose to do the right thing. Because he did the right thing, God made him healthy and strong. If you want to be healthy and strong, make good choices!

Lord, I choose to do the right things.
I won't listen to bad people. I know better. Amen.

King Nebuchadnezzar's Dream

DANIEL 2:17–49

No psychic can tell the mystery of your dream." Daniel spoke to King Nebuchadnezzar. "But there's a God in heaven who opens mysteries. You saw a huge, shining statue. Its head was made of gold. Its chest and arms were silver. Its middle and thighs were bronze. Its legs, iron. Its feet, part iron, part clay.

"As you watched, a stone was cut out, not by human hands. This stone hit the statue's feet of iron and clay. They broke into pieces. Then the entire statue broke into tiny pieces and blew away. The stone became a great mountain, filling the earth.

"Here is the dream's meaning: Your kingdom is the gold head. Later, another kingdom will come—the statue's silver shoulders and arms. Then a third kingdom of bronze will come. After that, a kingdom strong as iron will rise. Finally, a divided kingdom that is partly strong will rule. In those days God will set up His eternal kingdom. It will end all the earth's kingdoms and grow to fill the whole earth."

Nebuchadnezzar cried in awe, "Your God is the God of gods!"

Dreams and Visions

Then Arioch brought Daniel to the king in a hurry, and said to him, "I have found a man among those brought out of Judah who can tell the king the meaning of his dream!"
DANIEL 2:25

Most of our dreams don't mean anything. Some of them (like nightmares) come when we're afraid. Others, like silly dreams, might come because of something we ate before bedtime. But once in a while, God gives dreams as a message to His people. That's what happened in this story. Nebuchadnezzar's dream was a message straight from God. Wow! What would you do if God spoke to you through a dream or a vision? Would you tell others? Would you wake up wondering if it was really true?

Lord, I know I'm young, but You can still speak to me. I'm excited to hear all You have to say. Amen.

The Furnace of Blazing Fire

Daniel 3:1–30

Nebuchadnezzar made a golden statue ninety feet tall. An announcement was made to everyone to worship the statue or be thrown into the furnace.

Everyone worshiped the idol Nebuchadnezzar had set up. Everyone except Shadrach, Meshach, and Abednego, the friends of Daniel. They stood before the angry king.

"You must worship the golden statue I set up. If not, you'll be thrown into the furnace."

"O Nebuchadnezzar, we can only say this: We believe our God can save us from the furnace. If He doesn't, we still won't serve your gods. Nor will we worship your golden statue."

Nebuchadnezzar was so filled with rage that his face became hideous. "Heat the furnace seven times hotter than ever before," he commanded. His strongest guards tied up Shadrach, Meshach, and Abednego.

The furnace raged with heat and killed the guards. Shadrach, Meshach, and Abednego fell down into its flames.

Nebuchadnezzar was amazed looking into the furnace. "Didn't we tie three men and throw them into the furnace?"

"This is true, O king."

"But I see four men, untied, walking through the fire. They aren't hurt at all. One of them looks like a god." Then the king called: "Shadrach, Meshach, Abednego, servants of the most high God, come out!"

The three men came out to the king. They weren't burned, nor did they smell of fire.

"The God of Shadrach, Meshach, and Abednego is blessed!" the king declared. "No one may ever speak against their God."

God Is Your Protector

*Then Nebuchadnezzar came near the door where the fire
was burning, and said, "Shadrach, Meshach and Abed-nego,
servants of the Most High God, come out! Come here!"
So Shadrach, Meshach and Abed-nego came out of the fire.*
DANIEL 3:26

B oy, was this a hot story! Shadrach, Meshach, and Abednego wouldn't
bow down, so the king threw them into a fiery furnace. But the cool-
est thing happened! They walked around in the flames and didn't get
burned. God protected them. He was right there in the fire with them.
Did you know that God is right there with you when you go through
fiery trials? He's your protector and defender. Just like the three men
in the furnace, you will be safe in His care.

*Thanks for protecting me, Lord. I don't ever have to
worry because You'll take care of me. Amen.*

The Handwriting on the Wall

DANIEL 5:1-31

Belshazzar, the Babylonian king, was holding a great feast in honor of his false god. "Bring the gold and silver cups from Solomon's temple," Belshazzar commanded.

Suddenly a hand and fingers appeared. They wrote on the palace wall. King Belshazzar was so frightened, his knees knocked together. "Call the magicians and psychics!" he commanded.

"Read this writing," Belshazzar commanded the psychics. "If you do, I'll make you rich and famous." But they couldn't read the words the hand had written.

Then the queen said, "There's a certain man in your kingdom. He has the spirit of the holy gods. Let Daniel be called. He'll read these words."

Daniel was now an old man. Belshazzar said to him: "Read the handwriting on the wall, and I'll give you money and power."

"Keep your rewards. However, I'll read the writing for you, O king. God gave your father, Nebuchadnezzar, this kingdom. But Nebuchadnezzar became proud and was sent away. When he became humble, Nebuchadnezzar returned. But you also are proud. You haven't praised God who gives you this power. So God sent this hand to write on your wall.

"This is the writing: MENE means numbered; MENE again means numbered; TEKEL means weighed; UPHARSIN means divided. This is God's message: MENE, MENE—God has numbered the days of your kingdom. He has brought it to an end. TEKEL—you have been weighed on the scales. You are too light. UPHARSIN—your kingdom is divided. It's been given to the Medes and Persians."

That night, Cyrus and the Persians overran Babylon.

God Gets Our Attention

*All at once the fingers of a man's hand were seen writing
on the wall near the lamp-stand of the king's house.
And the king saw the back of the hand as it wrote.*
DANIEL 5:5

Have you ever ignored a friend or family member for so long that they thought you forgot about them? That's what happened in this story. Belshazzar was a proud man who didn't give God credit. So God had to do something unusual to get Belshazzar's attention. He wrote on the wall! Can you imagine how surprised Belshazzar must have been to see a hand appear and then write on the wall? Does God have your attention? Will He have to go out of His way to keep your mind from wandering?

*Lord, I don't want You to go out of Your way.
I'll pay attention! Amen.*

Daniel in the Lions' Den

DANIEL 6:11–28

Despite a new law against prayer, Daniel prayed toward Jerusalem three times daily. His enemies sought to frame him and asked King Darius about the death sentence concerning the law.

"There's someone, O king, who doesn't obey this law. It is Daniel from Judah. Before the law, he prayed three times a day. And he still does."

The king was very upset that Daniel had been accused. He spent the whole day trying to save his wise leader. That evening, the jealous leaders insisted that Daniel be punished.

So King Darius had to give the command. Daniel was brought and thrown into a den of lions. "You serve your God faithfully, Daniel," the king said. "I hope your God will save you from the lions." A stone was brought to seal the mouth of the cave. No one could let Daniel out of the lions' den.

After King Darius locked Daniel in the lions' den, he couldn't sleep. He was worried about Daniel. Early the next morning, the king ran to the lions' den.

He called, "Daniel, has God kept you safe from the lions?" The king thought he would hear the lions roar. But instead, he heard the voice of Daniel: "God sent His angel who shut the lions' mouths. He knew I had done nothing wrong. The lions haven't hurt me." So the king took Daniel out of the den. He punished the men who were so jealous of Daniel.

God Protects You

Then Daniel said to the king, "O king, live forever! My God sent
His angel and shut the lions' mouths. They have not hurt me,
because He knows that I am not guilty, and because
I have done nothing wrong to you, O king."
DANIEL 6:21-22

What would you do if someone told you that you weren't allowed to pray anymore? If you're like Daniel, you would probably go on praying anyway! Nothing can stop you from worshiping the Lord, after all. Daniel got in trouble because he kept praying. To punish him, the king threw him in a lions' den. But God performed a miracle! He watched over Daniel, and the lions never hurt him. Did you know that the same God who protected Daniel will protect you, too? It's true!

I want to be like Daniel, Lord! I won't ever stop praying. Amen.

Esther—Queen of Persia

ESTHER 2:5–5:8

At a grand banquet, a young Jewish woman named Esther was made queen of Persia. When the king wanted to see Esther, he sent for her. No one could go to the king's rooms without an invitation. Not even the queen.

At that time, Esther's uncle Mordecai was sitting at the palace gate. He overheard two men planning to kill the king. Mordecai sent word to Esther, who told King Ahasuerus. The men were captured and punished by death. Mordecai had saved the king's life. This was written in the history of Ahasuerus's empire.

"Go to the king." Queen Esther read Mordecai's message. "Plead with him to save your people."

Esther returned a message: "No one can go to the king's rooms without an invitation, or they'll die."

Mordecai told Esther: "You'll be killed like all the other Jews. You may be silent, Es-

ther, but God will rescue us another way. Who knows? Maybe you've become queen for just this time."

"Go then, Mordecai," wrote Esther. "Gather the Jews in Susa. Pray for me three days. I'll do the same. Then I'll go in to the king. If I die, I die."

Esther, dressed in her royal robes, stood in the king's court. The king, seeing her, held out the royal staff. This was his invitation. "What do you wish, Queen Esther? I'll give you anything."

"I've come to ask the king and Haman to dinner."

"Send word," he commanded. "Today Haman dines with the king and queen."

The three ate together. "What do you wish, Esther?" the king asked.

"Please, both of you, dine with me tomorrow. Then I'll tell you my desire."

Esther Loved Her People

And the king loved Esther more than all the women.
She found favor and kindness with him more than all the
young women, so that he set the queen's crown on
her head and made her queen instead of Vashti.
ESTHER 2:17

Esther loved her people, the Jews. She would do anything to protect them, so that's what she wanted the king's help with. What about you? Do you love your people—your parents, grandparents, brothers, sisters, and friends? They love you very much, and you love them, too. Esther was willing to risk everything to protect those she loved. Your family feels the same way about you. They will protect and love you at all costs. Doesn't it feel good to know your people are there for you when you need them?

Lord, thanks for sending me people who love me!
I love them, too. Amen.

Nehemiah—the City Builder

NEHEMIAH 1:1–2:9

In the days of Ezra lived a Jewish man named Nehemiah. Nehemiah served wine to the Persian king Artaxerxes. But Nehemiah loved Jerusalem more than the king's palace. Once, when men came visiting from Judea, he asked, "How is Jerusalem?"

"The people are very poor," Nehemiah was told. "No one respects them. Jerusalem's wall is broken down and her gates are burned."

Later, Nehemiah wrote, "When I heard these words, I sat down and wept. I said, 'O great and awesome God, hear my prayer. You promised to gather Your children to Jerusalem from under the farthest skies. O God, You bought them with Your great power. I will speak to the king about this. Cause him to grant my request.'

"When I served the king his wine, he noticed I was sad. 'You aren't sick,' he said. 'So why are you sad?' I breathed a silent prayer.

" 'The city where my ancestors are buried is in ruins,' I answered.

" 'What is it you want?'

" 'Send me to Judea where my ancestors are buried. Let me rebuild the city.' The king was happy to send me to Jerusalem."

God Rebuilds Things

*And I said to the king, "If it pleases the king, and if your servant
has found favor in your eyes, send me to Judah, to the
city of my fathers' graves. Let me build it again."*
NEHEMIAH 2:5

Nehemiah was sad when he learned that the wall around Jerusalem was broken down. How could the city ever heal with broken walls? He decided to do something about it. Nehemiah and his people rebuilt the wall until it was perfect again. Their hard work made God's heart very happy. Did you know that God loves to see things rebuilt? When things go wrong—when people make mistakes or get into arguments—God wants to make everything right again. He rebuilds broken situations and broken relationships. What a good God we serve!

*Thanks, Lord, for rebuilding broken things.
I'm glad You like to put things back together. Amen.*

The Building Begins

NEHEMIAH 2:11–3:32

Nehemiah and a group of horsemen rode one thousand miles to Jerusalem. He was there for three days. But Nehemiah told no one why God had sent him.

"I got up during the night," Nehemiah wrote. "A few men and I went out to look at the walls of Jerusalem. The way was too rough. So I left my horse and walked. The walls were in ruins and the gates burned to ash.

"I made my way back into the city. There I said, 'Come, let us rebuild the wall of Jerusalem. Then people around will respect us.' I told them what God had done with me. I also told them that the king had sent me. Then they said, 'Let's start building!'

"Soon people living in the lands around mocked us. 'What are you doing? Rebelling against the king?'

" 'The God of heaven will give us success,' I replied. 'We, His servants, are going to start building. You cannot share in this work.' "

Each family in Jerusalem agreed to build part of the wall. The high priest built one of the gates. A rich man built a long section. Others did a little. Some built much, some nothing.

Work as a Team

I answered them, "The God of heaven will make it go well for us. So we His servants will get up and build. But you have no share or right or anything to be remembered in Jerusalem."
NEHEMIAH 2:20

G od told Nehemiah to rebuild the wall around Jerusalem, and Nehemiah said, "Yes, Lord!" But it was a big job, and Nehemiah couldn't do it alone. He gathered a lot of men to help him. They were happy to be part of the team. Anytime you do a big job, you need helpers. The work is always easier when you do it as a team. Next time your sister needs to clean her room, offer to help her. She'll be happy to have you on her team! And remember, God is always on your team.

Thanks for being on my team, Lord!
You're the best worker of all. Amen.

The Building Is Completed

NEHEMIAH 4:1–6:16

Sanballat was a Samaritan. "What are these feeble Jews doing?" he mocked. Tobiah, an Ammonite, stood with Sanballat. "Any fox running on that wall would break it down," he laughed.

The people of Jerusalem rebuilt the wall to half its height. The Arabians and the Ammonites and the Ashdodites were very angry. They didn't want the city to be strong.

The Jews set guards day and night and continued to work. "Don't be afraid of them," said Nehemiah. "Remember the Lord is great and awesome. Fight for your families and homes."

Sanballat and Tobiah saw they couldn't attack. So they sent Nehemiah a message: "Come down. Meet us in the valley of Ono." They wanted to kill Nehemiah there.

"I'm doing a great work," he replied. "Why should this work stop while I meet with you?"

Finally, fifty-two days after it began, the work was finished. The gates were closed and guards were posted. The enemies around were afraid. They knew that the work had been done with God's help.

Finish What You Start

So the wall was finished on the twenty-fifth day of the month of Elul, in fifty-two days. When all those who hated us heard about it, all the nations around us were afraid and troubled. For they saw that this work had been done with the help of our God.
NEHEMIAH 6:15–16

When God tells you to do a job, it's best to do it right away. No dilly-dallying or lollygagging. Others are watching to make sure you do what you're told. And always remember to finish what you start. If you've been given the job of helping Mom clear the table, do your best. Don't stop until you're finished. If Dad asks you to pick up toys, pick up all of them, not just one or two. Be like Nehemiah and finish what you start.

Thanks for reminding me that I should finish what I start, Lord! Amen.

Zacharias Sees an Angel

LUKE 1:1–23

Just before Jesus Christ was born, King Herod ruled Judea for the Roman Empire. Herod had rebuilt the ancient Jewish temple. There a priest helped with the worship. His name was Zacharias; his wife was Elizabeth.

One day Zacharias was ministering in the Holy Place. Outside, the court was full of worshipers. Suddenly, he saw an angel. Zacharias was terrified.

"Fear not," the angel said. "God has heard your prayer. Elizabeth will have a baby boy. You'll name him John. Many will rejoice when he's born. He'll have Elijah's spirit and turn many to the Lord."

"How will I know this is true?" questioned Zacharias. "I'm an old man, and my wife is old, too."

"I'm Gabriel," said the angel. "God sent me to give you good news. But you don't believe me. I said that this will happen, but you won't speak until it does."

When Zacharias came out, the people could tell he'd seen a vision. He tried to signal to them, but they couldn't understand. When his service in the temple was over, Zacharias went home.

Speechless

The angel said to him, "Zacharias, do not be afraid.
Your prayer has been heard. Your wife Elizabeth will
give birth to a son. You are to name him John."
LUKE 1:13

After the angel gave Zacharias the good news, he was speechless. He couldn't say a word! Has that ever happened to you? Maybe you were so excited, you were speechless. You didn't know what to say. There will be times when God wants us to be silent, to just listen—to others and to Him. Do you know how to be silent? It's not easy, is it? We love to talk, after all. Today, why not test yourself? Go fifteen minutes without speaking a word. Can you do it? What did you learn in the silence?

Lord, I will be silent and listen for Your still, small voice.
I won't be the one doing all the talking, Father. Amen.

Gabriel Greets Mary

LUKE 1:26–38

"This is what God has done for me!" praised Elizabeth. She had just learned she and Zacharias were to have a baby.

Next, God sent the angel Gabriel to Nazareth. This town is in Galilee, north of Judea. Living there was a girl named Mary, who was to wed Joseph.

"Greetings," Gabriel said. "You are God's favorite woman. God is with you."

"What kind of speaking is this?" Mary wondered.

"Don't be afraid," Gabriel continued. "You're going to have a baby boy. You'll call His name Jesus. He'll be called the Son of God."

You Are Highly Favored

The angel came to her and said, "You are honored very
much. You are a favored woman. The Lord is with you.
You are chosen from among many women."
LUKE 1:28

The Bible says that Mary was highly favored. This means she was one of God's favorites. Have you ever wondered what it would be like to be the favorite kid? The truth is, we're all God's favorites. He loves each of us so much and wants us to know how much we matter to Him. When you're highly favored, God sometimes asks you to do extra-special tasks for Him. Mary was given one of the most amazing tasks of all—giving birth to baby Jesus!

Lord, thank You for showing me Your favor!
It feels so good to be blessed by You. Amen.

The Birth of John the Baptist

LUKE 1:39–80

Hello, Elizabeth." Mary had come to see her cousin Elizabeth. When Elizabeth heard Mary's voice, her baby jumped inside her. She was filled with the Holy Spirit.

"Mary! You are the most blessed of all women," Elizabeth exclaimed. "Your baby is blessed, too. Why has my Lord's mother come to see me? When I heard your voice, my baby jumped for joy inside me."

Some months later, Elizabeth's baby, John, was born. He would grow up in the wilderness—a Nazirite priest for God. This was the last prophet—John the Baptist.

Holy Cousins

Then they talked to his father with their hands to find out what he would name the child. He asked for something to write on. He wrote, "His name is John." They were all surprised and wondered about it.
LUKE 1:62–63

John and Jesus were very special cousins. One of them, Jesus, was the Savior of the world. The other, John, was an anointed priest and prophet. What a team they must have been! Do you have any cousins or friends you're really close to? It's wonderful to be close to someone who has a strong faith like you do. You can pray together, talk about Jesus, and have fun playing together. Today, thank God for your cousins and friends.

Lord, thank You for my cousins, especially the ones who believe in You. They are such gifts to me, Father. Amen.

The Birth of Jesus Christ

MATTHEW 1:18–21; LUKE 2:1–7

Joseph was a carpenter in Nazareth. He was soon to be Mary's husband. One night he had a dream. In it an angel spoke: "Joseph, take Mary as your wife. The Child in her is from the Holy Spirit. When He's born, call him Jesus. He'll save His people from their sins."

In those days, Emperor Augustus Caesar commanded that his people be counted. To do this, everyone went to their hometown. For Mary and Joseph, this was Bethlehem. Bethlehem was also King David's hometown.

It was a long journey from Nazareth to Bethlehem. Mary, who was almost ready to have her baby, traveled with Joseph. They went down the hills in Galilee to the Jordan River. Then they followed the river to Judea. Up in the Judean hills, they came to Bethlehem. The town was full of people who had come to be counted. An inn was there, but it was full of people.

Suddenly, Mary had to give birth. So they went into a stable. Here Mary had her Child, Jesus. She wrapped Him in a blanket and put Him to sleep in a feed trough.

A Journey Ends in Celebration!

*Her first son was born. She put cloth around Him and laid Him
in a place where cattle are fed. There was no room for
them in the place where people stay for the night.*
LUKE 2:7

Have you ever been on a long road trip in the car? Maybe Mom and Dad woke you up extra early and said, "Come on! We've got to get on the road!" So you settled into the car with your pillow and a few toys and sang songs as you traveled down the road. Maybe your journey ended at your grandmother's house or the home of a friend. Maybe you arrived just in time for a big party. That's how Mary must have felt when she arrived in Bethlehem and gave birth to the King of kings. What a celebration!

*Lord, thank You for the birth of Your Son, Jesus.
Best birthday ever! Amen.*

The Angel's Announcement

LUKE 2:8–20

That night, shepherds guarded their sheep near Bethlehem. Suddenly, they were surrounded with light. An angel stood there. The shepherds were terrified.

"Don't be afraid. I've come to give you good news. Today, in Bethlehem, Christ the Lord has been born. You'll find Him wrapped in a blanket, sleeping in a feed trough."

Suddenly, the sky was filled with angels praising God. "Glory to God in heaven! On earth, peace and goodwill."

"Let's go to Bethlehem and see this wonderful thing."

And they did. There they found Mary, Joseph, and Jesus, as the angel had said.

Obedient Shepherds

The angels went from the shepherds back to heaven. The shepherds
said to each other, "Let us go now to Bethlehem and see what
has happened. The Lord has told us about this."
LUKE 2:15

What a night that must have been! The shepherds were guarding their sheep on the hillside late at night when a bright light lit up the sky. Can you imagine how frightened they must have been? Suddenly a host of angels started praising God. Wow! What would you do if you saw an angel? Would you be frightened? Would you join their song? The shepherds listened and obeyed what the angels told them to do. They traveled to Bethlehem and found baby Jesus with His mother and adoptive father.

Lord, I want to be obedient like the shepherds.
When You tell me where to go, I will go. Amen.

The Rising Star of Christ

MATTHEW 2:1–14

In the East, far from Bethlehem, lived some very wise men who studied the stars. They traveled to Jerusalem to ask one question: "Where is the Child who's born to be King of the Jews? We saw His star rise in the sky, so we came to honor Him."

When King Herod heard this, he was afraid he would lose his kingdom. Secretly, Herod spoke to the wise men from the East: "When you've found the Child, tell me. I want to honor Him, too."

When they had heard the king, the men set out. There, ahead of them, went the star they had seen rising. It finally stopped over a house. The travelers were overcome by joy.

The joyous men entered the house and saw the Child with Mary. They knelt down with reverence. Then, opening their treasure chests, they offered Jesus gifts. They gave Him precious gold, frankincense, and myrrh.

When the men left, they didn't return to Herod. In a dream, one of them had been warned not to do this. So they traveled back to their land by another road.

Joseph saw an angel in a dream. "Hurry away to Egypt," the angel said. "Herod wants to kill the Child."

That night the family left for Egypt.

Very Special Gifts

They went into the house and found the young Child with Mary,
His mother. Then they got down before Him and worshiped
Him. They opened their bags of riches and gave
Him gifts of gold and perfume and spices.
MATTHEW 2:11

Happy birthday, Jesus! When the wise men came to visit the young Child, they brought very special gifts—gold, frankincense, and myrrh. It's always fun to receive gifts, but it's even more fun to give. If you had visited Jesus, what gifts would you have brought? Did you know that the very best gift you can give Jesus is your heart? It's what He wants most of all.

Lord Jesus, today I give You my heart. I make You Lord and Savior
of my life. Thank You for coming as a baby and dying on the
cross. Please forgive me of my sins, I pray. Amen.

In His Father's House

Luke 2:40–52

Jesus grew and became strong. He was full of wisdom, and God preferred [favored] Him.

When Jesus was twelve years old, His family went to Jerusalem for the Passover. Afterward, they started home, but the boy Jesus stayed behind in Jerusalem. When they couldn't find Him, they returned to Jerusalem. There they searched for Jesus.

After three days, they found Him in the temple. The teachers were amazed at His understanding and answers. When His parents saw Him, they were surprised. His mother said, "Child, why have You treated us like this? Your father and I have been looking for You. We've been worried sick."

"Why were you searching for Me?" Jesus asked her. "Didn't you know that I would be in My Father's house?" But they didn't understand His meaning.

Then Jesus went down with them from Jerusalem. They returned to Nazareth, and He obeyed them. His mother always remembered the things He did and said.

Jesus grew in wisdom and in years. He was preferred by God and the people.

A Wise Boy

They thought Jesus was with the others of the group.
They walked for one day. Then they looked for
Him among their family and friends.
LUKE 2:44

Jesus loved to spend time with the teachers in the temple, learning all He could. He loved it so much that He didn't want to leave! What about you? Do you like to go to church and learn about God? What's your favorite thing about it? Who are your favorite teachers? Have they taught you how to pray? Are you learning how to be obedient and how to stick close to God? Going to church is a wonderful way to learn about being a Christian.

God, thank You for my teachers. They teach me
such great things about You! Amen.

The Work of John the Baptist

LUKE 3:1–22; MATTHEW 3:13–17

John, the son of Elizabeth and Zacharias, lived in the wilderness. Zacharias's son was also Israel's last prophet. When he was thirty, God sent him to the Jewish people. He told them to turn from sin and be forgiven. John baptized those who turned from sin in the Jordan River.

John the Baptist wore rough clothes woven from camel hair and a leather belt. He ate dried grasshoppers and wild honey from the trees. John's words were different, too. He said: "Turn from sin and do right. The kingdom of heaven is nearby. Its King will soon be here."

"I wonder if he's Christ?" everyone wondered about John the Baptist.

"I baptize you with water," he answered. "The One who's coming is greater than I am. He'll baptize you with the Holy Spirit and fire." John was speaking of Jesus.

Jesus came to be baptized by John. But John said, "You should baptize me."

"It's proper for us to do this," Jesus answered. "We'll be doing what's right."

John baptized Jesus. Just then, God's Spirit came down like a dove. And God spoke: "This is My Son whom I love. He pleases Me."

Turn Around

But John said to all of them, "I baptize you with water.
There is One coming Who is greater than I. I am not good
enough to get down and help Him take off His shoes.
He will baptize you with the Holy Spirit and with fire."
LUKE 3:16

Have you ever spun around in circles? The Bible tells us that God wants us to turn around—to go in the opposite direction from sin. Not sure how that works? Let's say you're having a fight with your sister. In the middle of the fight you think, *I shouldn't be fighting with her. It makes God sad.* So you stop and say, "I'm sorry!" You go the opposite direction. That's what John the Baptist was telling the people to do. . .to turn from sin and go the opposite way.

Today I will turn away from doing what's wrong
and choose to obey, Lord. Amen.

The Devil Tempts Jesus

Luke 4:1–11

The Spirit of God led Jesus into the wilderness. There He was tempted by the devil. When He was hungry, the devil came. "If You're God's Son, make these stones into bread."

"One doesn't only live on bread. God's words are food as well."

The devil took Him to the temple roof. "The angels won't let You get hurt," he tempted. "So jump to the ground."

"It's written, 'Don't put God to the test.' "

"I'll give You all of earth's kingdoms; worship me!" commanded Satan.

"Get away, Satan! The Bible says, 'Worship and serve only God.' "

The Enemy

He was tempted by the devil for forty days and He ate nothing during that time. After that He was hungry.
LUKE 4:2

Did you know that we have a very real enemy? His name is Satan (the devil), and he's always trying to trick us into doing bad things. He whispers in our ear: "Go ahead and hit your brother. He deserves it." Or sometimes he says, "It's okay to lie to Mom. She won't know." But Jesus doesn't want us to listen to the devil. We have to stand firm and say, "No, Devil! I'm going to follow Jesus, not you!" Don't choose to go the wrong way or you'll end up in trouble!

Jesus, I will do my best not to listen when the devil tries to trick me, but I need Your help! Amen.

Jesus Finds His Followers

JOHN 1:29–41

When the devil left Jesus alone, angels came and cared for Him. Then He went back to where John was by the Jordan River. John saw Jesus coming toward him. "Look! It's the Lamb of God who takes away the world's sin. This is the One I said was greater than I am. I've seen this, and now I tell you: this is the Son of God!"

The next morning, John was standing with two of his followers. Jesus walked by. John shouted, "Look, here is the Lamb of God!" His two followers heard this and followed Jesus.

Jesus turned around and said, "What are you looking for?"

"Teacher," they replied, "where do You live?"

"Come and see."

One man, Andrew, found his brother, Simon, and said, "We've found the Christ!" He brought Simon to Jesus.

Jesus looked at Simon and said, "You are John's son, Simon. But your new name is Peter."

The next day, Jesus went to Galilee. He said to Philip, "Follow Me."

Later, Jesus met Nathaniel, who said: "Teacher, You're the Son of God! You're the King of Israel!"

You Have a Team

Andrew, Simon Peter's brother, was one of the two who had heard John's words and had followed Jesus. The first thing he did was to find his brother Simon. He said to him, "We have found the Christ!"
JOHN 1:40–41

Jesus had a group of followers, called His disciples. They were His team. A team is a group of people who are always on your side. They love, defend, and protect you. Do you have a team? Think about the people you see all the time. You have family, friends, neighbors, and even people at church who love you and will protect you, no matter what. So don't forget to pray for your team and to thank God for them!

*God, thank You for my team. I'm so glad
I have people on my side. Amen.*

"You'll Fish for People"

MATTHEW 4:18–22

Jesus walked by the Sea of Galilee. There He saw Peter and Andrew again. They were casting a net into the sea because they were fishermen. He said to them, "Follow Me and you'll fish for people."

Right away, they left their nets and followed Him. Farther down the beach, Jesus saw two other brothers. James and John were in a fishing boat with their father, Zebedee. They were mending their nets. Jesus called to them. At once, they left their father in the boat and followed Him.

Follow Jesus

Jesus said to them, "Follow Me. I will make you fish for men!"
At once they left their nets and followed Him.
MATTHEW 4:19–20

J esus told the fishermen to follow Him. What did He mean by that? Were they supposed to leave their families, their homes, and travel with Him? Some of them did exactly that. They became His disciples. God wants you to follow Him, too, but He's not asking you to leave your family or change where you live. You can stay right where you are! To follow Him means that you give Him your heart and do the things the Bible says. Following Jesus is a great adventure. You'll get the best friend ever!

I will follow You forever, Jesus! I love to play
follow-the-leader with You. Amen.

The Miracle at the Wedding

JOHN 2:1–11

J esus and His followers went to a town called Cana. There was a wedding in that town. Everyone was having fun and eating a big meal. But before the meal was over, they ran out of wine. Mary, Jesus' mother, knew He could help. Mary said to Jesus, "They have no wine." He said, "It is not time for Me to do miracles." But Mary told the people, "Do what He tells you."

Six big stone jars were standing there. They each could hold as much water as a bathtub. Jesus said, "Fill those jars with water." The servants did what He said. Then Jesus told them, "Take some of it to the leader of this wedding." So they dipped some water out of the jars. It had changed to wine.

The leader of the wedding was surprised. He spoke to the bridegroom. "This wine is better than any you have served so far. You kept the best wine until last."

This was the first time Jesus did something to prove He was the Son of God. When His followers saw it, they believed in Jesus even more.

Prove It!

*This was the first powerful work Jesus did. It was done
in Cana of Galilee where He showed His power.
His followers put their trust in Him.*
JOHN 2:11

Have you ever heard someone say, "Prove it!" Maybe you tell your
mom you love her and she says, "Prove it!" So you give her a kiss
or a hug. When we prove something, people know for sure. They can
trust that what we're saying really is true. That's what happened at this
wedding. There were party guests who didn't know that Jesus was the
Son of God. When He performed the miracle of turning the water into
wine, He proved it. Who else could perform a miracle, after all? After
that, everyone trusted in Him.

*Lord, thank You for proving how much You love me.
I love You, and I trust You, too! Amen.*

The Woman at Jacob's Well

JOHN 4:7-42

Jesus traveled from Judea to Samaria. About noontime, Jesus rested by Jacob's well, and His followers went to buy food. A woman came to the well to draw water. "Give Me a drink," Jesus said.

"You're a Jew," she said. "I'm a Samaritan. Jews don't share with Samaritans."

"You don't know who's asking you for a drink. If you did, you'd ask Me for a drink. Then I'd give you living water. Whoever drinks water from this well," Jesus said, "will get thirsty again. But when I give you water, the well is inside of you. It bubbles up to give you eternal life."

"Sir," the woman said, "please give me this water. Then I'll never thirst again. I won't have to come to this well."

"The real worshipers worship the Father in spirit and in truth," Jesus answered.

Then the woman said, "I know Christ is coming. When He does, He'll teach us everything."

"I'm speaking to you. I'm Christ."

Just then, Jesus' followers came back with the food. They were surprised that Jesus was talking with this Samaritan woman. She left her water jug at the well and hurried back to town. "Come and see a man who told me everything I've ever done! Could He be Christ?"

Many people in that town believed in Jesus because of the woman. Jesus stayed there two days. Many more believed because they heard His words.

Never Thirst Again

Jesus said to her, "Whoever drinks this water will be thirsty again. Whoever drinks the water that I will give him will never be thirsty. The water that I will give him will become in him a well of life that lasts forever."
JOHN 4:13–14

Jesus told the woman at the well that if she drank His water, she would never thirst again. Seems impossible, doesn't it? We get thirsty all the time. But Jesus wasn't talking about ordinary water. He wanted this woman to give her heart to Him. When we give our hearts to Jesus, He satisfies us. We don't need to go looking for love anywhere else. So give your heart to Him, and you will never need to look for love in other places.

Lord, I get it! When I give You my heart, You will satisfy me completely. I'm so happy to be Your child. Amen.

"Let Down Your Nets for Fish"

LUKE 5:1–11

Once Jesus was beside the Sea of Galilee. Nearby were two fishing boats, belonging to Peter and Andrew and James and John. These young disciples were nearby washing their nets. Jesus stepped into Peter's boat and sat teaching the crowds.

Jesus finished teaching. "Peter," He said, "put out into deep water and let down your nets for fish."

"Master," Peter answered, "we've worked all night long and caught nothing. But if You say so, I'll let down the nets." When they did, they caught so many fish their nets were breaking. Peter signaled James and John, who came and filled both boats to overflowing!

Overwhelmed with God's wonder, he fell down and cried, "Go away from me, Lord. I'm a sinful man!"

"Don't be afraid," Jesus comforted Peter. "From now on, you'll catch people." The young men left their boats and all they had and followed Jesus.

Fishing for People

Simon said to Him, "Teacher, we have worked all night and we have caught nothing. But because You told me to, I will let the net down."
LUKE 5:5

Jesus told the fishermen to put down their nets on the other side of the boat. When they did, they caught lots of fish! Jesus then said something strange. He said: "From now on, you'll catch people." What do you think He meant by that? Jesus was trying to tell the fishermen that they were going to share the message of God's love with people everywhere. Many people who heard the message became believers. (Did you know that giving your heart to Jesus is the very best catch of all? It's true!)

*Lord, I'm so glad You caught my heart. I'm Your child forever.
Time to go fishing! Amen.*

The Power to Forgive Sins

LUKE 5:17–26

Pharisees and teachers came from every village in Galilee. They came all the way from Jerusalem to Capernaum. Jesus was teaching them, and God's power was with Him to heal.

Just then, men came carrying a paralyzed man on a bed. They tried to bring him into the house to Jesus. But it was too crowded. So they went up on the roof and took off some roof tiles. They let the paralyzed man down into the house. There he was in front of Jesus in the middle of the crowd.

Jesus saw that these men had faith. "Friend," He said, "your sins are forgiven you."

The Pharisees questioned this. "He's speaking heresy," they whispered. "No one can forgive sins except God."

Jesus knew their thoughts. "Why do you question this? Is it easier to say, 'Your sins are forgiven,' or 'Stand up and walk'? I want you to know that I have the power to forgive sins." Then Jesus spoke to the paralyzed man: "Stand up, take your bed, and go home." And the man did this, praising God.

Everyone was amazed and praised God. "We've seen great things today," they said.

Friends Who Go the Distance

But they could not find a way to take him in because of so many people. They made a hole in the roof over where Jesus stood. Then they let the bed with the sick man on it down before Jesus.
LUKE 5:19

Wow, what awesome friends these were! They cared so much about this man that they were willing to climb onto a roof, cut a hole, and lower their friend's sickbed down into the room below so that Jesus could heal him. That's how much they cared. Do you have good friends? Do they pray for you? God wants you to be the kind of friend who will take care of others and pray for their needs.

Lord, thank You for my friends. I'm so glad they pray for me. I promise to pray for them, too. Amen.

Jesus Teaches on the Mountain

Matthew 5:1–9

Jesus saw the huge crowds on the mountain. His disciples came, too, and He taught them:

> The poor in spirit are blessed because theirs is the kingdom of heaven.
> The meek are blessed because they'll inherit the earth.
> People who are hungry to do right are blessed because they'll be filled.
> People who have mercy are blessed because they'll be given mercy.
> The pure in heart are blessed because they'll see God.
> Peacemakers are blessed because they'll be called children of God.

No Pity Parties

*Jesus saw many people. He went up on the mountain
and sat down. His followers came to Him.*
MATTHEW 5:1

Sometimes we feel bad for ourselves when things go wrong. We throw a pity party. We think, *Why me, Lord? Why is everything going wrong? I didn't do anything to deserve this.* It doesn't seem fair. But Jesus reminds us in this sermon that He's blessing us even when we're poor or sick or hungry. The truth is, God loves and blesses us no matter what we're going through. So even if you're having a hard day (and everyone does), remember that He is still loving and blessing you.

*I do have hard days sometimes, Lord, but I won't throw a pity party.
I'm going to try to remember that You are still blessing me. Amen.*

Sins and Love
LUKE 7:36-50

A Pharisee named Simon invited Jesus to supper. There, a woman came with a beautiful little jar of perfume. She was weeping at Jesus' feet. This was a well-known sinful woman who lived in town. Jesus' feet were bathed in her tears. Then the woman dried them with her hair. As this sinful woman kissed Jesus' feet, she anointed them with perfume.

"I don't think this man's a prophet," Simon said to himself. "If He were, He'd know who's touching Him. She's a sinner."

Jesus spoke up. "Simon, I want to tell you a story.

"Two people owed another man money. The first owed five hundred dollars. The other owed fifty dollars. Neither of them could pay. So he told them both they didn't need to pay him back. Which one loved him more?"

Simon the Pharisee answered, "I suppose the one who owed the most money."

Jesus said to him, "You're right. I came to your house. Did you give me water to wash My feet? No. Do you see this woman, Simon? She bathed My feet in tears and wiped them with her hair. You didn't greet me with a kiss. But since I came, she hasn't stopped kissing My feet. You didn't anoint My head with oil. But she has anointed My feet. I tell you, her many sins are forgiven. But the one who's done little to forgive loves little."

A Precious Gift

There was a woman in the city who was a sinner.
She knew Jesus was eating in the house of the proud religious
law-keeper. She brought a jar of special perfume.
LUKE 7:37

The woman who came to Jesus brought a jar of valuable perfume, which she poured onto His feet. That might seem a little strange to you, but it was her way of offering Him her best, her most precious gift. What can you give to Jesus today? What is your most precious gift? It's your heart! When you pour out your love, when you tell Jesus that He can live in your heart, you've given Him the most precious gift of all.

Lord Jesus, today I give You my most precious gift, my heart!
I pour it out like perfume. Thank You for loving me. Amen.

The Wind and the Sea Obey Jesus

MARK 4:35–41

At evening, Jesus said, "Let's cross to the other side." With other boats, the disciples rowed across the Sea of Galilee. A big storm came up. Waves beat into the boat. It was about to be swamped. But Jesus was asleep in the stern of the boat.

They awakened Him. "Teacher, don't You care that we're all about to drown?"

He woke up and rebuked the wind. Speaking to the sea, Jesus said, "Peace! Be still." The wind stopped, and there was dead calm on the water.

"Why are you afraid?" He asked them. "Do you still have no faith?"

They were filled with great awe. "Who is this?" they asked each other. "Even the wind and the sea obey Him."

A Scary Night

He got up and spoke sharp words to the wind. He said to the sea, "Be quiet! Be still." At once the wind stopped blowing. There were no more waves.
MARK 4:39

Have you ever been scared? Maybe a storm blew in one night while you were sleeping and thunder shook your house. When you're really scared, what do you do? Even in your scariest times, God wants you to be at peace and to trust Him. In today's Bible story, Jesus took one look at those big waves and said, "Peace, be still!" Right away, the storm calmed down. You can look at the scary moments in your life and say, "Peace, be still!" too. God will calm your heart as you trust in Him.

Thanks for reminding me that I can feel peace even during scary times, Lord. I put my trust in You. Amen.

"Who Touched Me?"

MARK 5:22–34

Again they crossed the sea in the boat. On the other shore, a big crowd gathered. A Jewish leader named Jairus came forward and fell at Jesus' feet. "My little daughter is about to die. Come and touch her so she will live." So Jesus went with him. The crowd followed and pushed in on Him.

In the crowd was a woman who'd been bleeding for twelve years. She had spent all her money on doctors. They couldn't help her; in fact, she grew worse. She had heard about Jesus and came up behind Him. She said to herself, *If I touch His clothes, I'll be healed.* She touched His cloak. Instantly, her bleeding stopped. The woman knew she was healed.

Jesus also knew something had happened. He had felt power go out from Him. "Who touched Me?" He asked.

"The crowd is pushing in on You," said His disciples. "How can You ask, 'Who touched Me?' " But He looked all around for who had done it.

The woman came to Him in fear and trembling. She told Him the whole story. "Daughter," He said, "your faith has made you well. Go in peace and be healed."

A Miracle of Healing

She heard about Jesus and went among the people who were following Him. She touched His coat. For she said to herself, "If I can only touch His coat, I will be healed."
MARK 5:27–28

Have you ever witnessed a miracle? When God does something so over-the-top, so amazing, you know it's a miracle. Humans can't perform miracles. They're impossible! Only God can do it. In this story, Jesus healed a woman of a terrible sickness. The doctors couldn't make her well, but Jesus could. Did you know God wants you to have faith to believe in miracles? It's true! If you know someone who's really sick, or going through a hard time, don't forget to pray. God just might work a miracle!

God, I believe in miracles! My faith is strong, Lord.
I put my trust in You and believe for the impossible. Amen.

"She's Not Dead; She's Sleeping"

MARK 5:35–43

Your daughter's dead, Jairus," people said. "Don't trouble the teacher." But Jesus overheard.

"Don't fear, Jairus," He said. "Only believe."

Jesus wouldn't let anyone follow Him to Jairus's house. Only Peter, James, and John went along. There, people loudly wailed.

"Why so much noise? She's not dead; she's sleeping." They laughed at Jesus. He put them outside. With her parents and the disciples, Jesus went to the girl. He took her hand. "Little girl, get up." She arose and walked around. They were overcome with amazement. "Don't tell anyone," Jesus ordered. "And give her something to eat."

From Death to Life

He took the girl by the hand and said, "Little girl, I say to you, get up!" At once the girl got up and walked. She was twelve years old. They were very much surprised and wondered about it.
MARK 5:41–42

This is one of the greatest miracles of all time! Jesus spoke to a dead person and she came back to life. Wow! Is that even possible? With God, nothing is impossible, even life after death. He spoke the words "Little girl, get up!" and she got up! (Can you imagine how surprised her parents must have been?) What would you do if you witnessed a miracle like this? One day you will! Jesus will take you to heaven and you will live forever with Him.

What a miracle worker You are, Lord! I'm so glad there's life after death. One day I'll live in heaven with You! Amen.

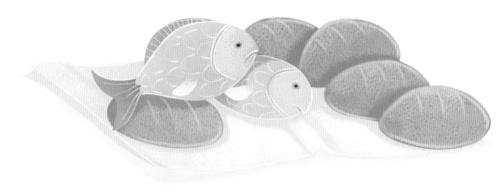

Jesus Feeds the Crowds

MATTHEW 14:13–18

Jesus heard John the Baptist had been killed. So He retreated in a boat to a secluded place. The people followed on foot around the Sea of Galilee. So when Jesus came ashore, He saw huge crowds waiting. There He cared for them.

"It's late," said the disciples. "Send them away for food."

"They don't need to leave," said Jesus. "You give them food."

"All we have is five loaves and two fish."

Taking these, Jesus looked up to heaven. He blessed and broke the loaves. Then everyone ate their fill. They filled twelve baskets with leftovers.

God Multiplies!

They said to Him, "We have only five loaves of bread and two fish." Jesus said, "Bring them to Me."
MATTHEW 14:17–18

Do you know what it feels like to be hungry? What if you had no food to eat? The people in this story were very hungry, but there was no food to give them. Only one little boy in the crowd had food—five loaves of bread and two little fish. He brought the food to Jesus, who blessed it (prayed for it). And guess what happened? The loaves and fish multiplied. There was enough food to feed thousands of people. Wow, what a miracle!

Lord, You're great at multiplying. You take a little and turn it into a lot! You're so awesome. Amen.

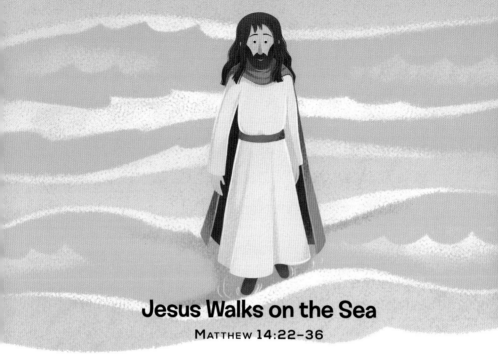

Jesus Walks on the Sea

MATTHEW 14:22-36

After feeding the crowds, Jesus sent the disciples back to the boat. He went up the mountain alone to pray. By evening, the boat was far from land. The disciples struggled to sail against high waves and strong winds. At dawn, Jesus came to them walking on the sea.

"It's a ghost!" they cried out in fear.

"Take heart, it is I," Jesus said. "Don't be afraid."

Peter answered, "Lord, command me to walk on the water."

He said, "Come."

So Peter started walking on the water toward Jesus. But when Peter felt the wind, he began to sink. Peter cried out, "Lord, save me!"

Instantly, Jesus reached and caught him. "You have so little faith," Jesus said. "Why did you doubt?" Back in the boat, the wind stopped.

"Truly, You are the Son of God," they said. And the disciples worshiped Him.

When the boat came to land, the sick were brought to Jesus. "Just let us touch the edge of your cloak," the people begged. All those who touched it were healed.

Keep Your Eyes on Jesus

Peter said to Jesus, "If it is You, Lord, tell me to come to You on the water." Jesus said, "Come!" Peter got out of the boat and walked on the water to Jesus.
MATTHEW 14:28–29

W alking on water is impossible. It's absolutely, totally, without a doubt impossible. But Jesus did it! Then He called Peter to walk on the water with Him. Peter tried, but he started sinking. Then Jesus said, "Keep your eyes on Me, Peter!" Peter did, and he walked on water, too! That's how it is with us when we're in trouble. We need to keep our eyes on Jesus and keep our faith strong, and miracles will happen.

I'm going to keep my eyes on You, Lord, no matter what. You can work miracles! Amen.

"Forgive Others from Your Heart"

MATTHEW 18:21–35

Peter asked, "How often should I forgive someone? Seven times?"

Jesus answered, "Not seven times; I tell you: seventy-seven times.

"Once a king's servant owed him ten million dollars. He couldn't pay. The king ordered, 'Sell this man and his family into slavery to pay his debt.'

"The servant begged, 'Be patient. I'll pay you everything.'

"Pitying him, the king said, 'You don't have to pay.'

"Later, a man owed the servant one hundred dollars. 'Pay me what you owe,' he demanded. The man pleaded, 'Have patience. I'll pay you!' But the servant put him in jail until he could pay.

"Other servants saw this and told the king. The king said to the servant, 'You wicked servant, I forgave you your debt because you begged me to. I had mercy on you. Shouldn't you have had mercy on that man?' The king sent him to prison until he'd paid his debt.

"Peter, the lesson is this: My Father is like the king in this story. You are like the servant. So always forgive others from your heart."

It's Better to Forgive

Then Peter came to Jesus and said, "Lord, how many times
may my brother sin against me and I forgive him,
up to seven times?" Jesus said to him, "I tell you,
not seven times but seventy times seven!"
MATTHEW 18:21–22

Has anyone ever hurt your feelings? Maybe your friend said something mean or your sister did something rude to you. When people hurt your feelings, you probably don't feel like forgiving them. It's easier to stay mad! But you need to forgive anyway. The Bible says that forgiving is the best way to live. When you forgive others, then God forgives you for the bad things you've done. That's a great thing to remember.

Thank You for forgiving me for the bad things I've done.
I will forgive others, Lord. Amen.

The Camel in the Needle's Eye

MATTHEW 19:16–26

Later, a young man asked, "What shall I do to have eternal life?"

"Keep the commandments," Jesus answered.

"I've kept all ten. What else is there?"

"Sell everything. Give the money to the poor. Come and follow Me."

When the young man heard this, he walked away sadly. He was very rich.

Jesus spoke to His disciples: "Can a camel go through a needle's eye? That's how hard it is for the rich to enter the kingdom."

"So who can be saved?" they wondered.

"To you, it's impossible," He answered. "But God can do anything."

Some Things Aren't Easy

"Again I tell you, it is easier for a camel to go through the eye of a needle than for a rich man to get into the holy nation of heaven."
MATTHEW 19:24

What do you think Jesus meant when He told the disciples that it was easier for a camel to go through the eye of a needle than for a rich man to enter heaven? Was He talking about a real camel and a real needle? Jesus was saying that some things are really, really hard. Maybe you know what that feels like. Some things are hard for you, too. But God wants you to try, even when things are super-duper hard. Give it your all. Don't give up. Give it your best shot, kid!

Lord, I won't give up! I'll keep trying, even when things seem impossible. With Your help, I can do it. Amen.

The One Thing That's Needed

LUKE 10:38-42

One day Jesus went to Martha and Mary's house. Mary had once anointed Jesus' feet and wiped them with her hair. She enjoyed sitting at the Lord's feet listening to Him talk. Martha was very busy with other things in the house. She said to Jesus, "My sister has left all the work for me to do. Does that bother You at all?"

"Martha, Martha," He answered, "you're worried about so many things. But there's only one thing that's really needed. Mary has chosen to love Me, and that won't be taken from her."

Busy, Busy!

*"Only a few things are important, even just one. Mary has chosen
the good thing. It will not be taken away from her."*
LUKE 10:42

Martha was a busy, busy lady! When Jesus came to her house, she wanted everything to be perfect! She probably cleaned and prepared food and made sure everything was just right, totally spick-and-span. Her sister Mary wasn't much help. Mary just wanted to hang out with Jesus, to sit at His feet and listen to Him talk. Mary's unhelpfulness with the housework made Martha mad. But guess what? Jesus wanted Martha to sit and rest, too. Sometimes it's more important to sit quietly with Jesus than to stay busy.

*Sometimes I'm busy, busy, busy—just like Martha from this story.
Thanks for reminding me that You want me to slow down
so You can spend time with me, Lord. Amen.*

Mud on a Blind Man's Eyes

JOHN 9:1-9

As Jesus walked in Jerusalem, He saw a blind man. This man had been born blind. His disciples asked this question: "Teacher, whose fault was it that he is blind? Did his parents sin? Was it his sin that caused this?"

"He was born blind for a reason," Jesus answered. "This has nothing to do with anyone's sin. God wants to work in him. We must do God's work while it is day. Night is coming when no one can work. As long as I'm in the world, I'm the light of the world."

Then Jesus spit on the ground. He made mud with His spit and spread it on the man's eyes. "Go wash your eyes in the Siloam pool," Jesus told him. The blind man went to the pool with mud on his eyes. He washed, and for the first time in his life, he could see. His neighbors had always seen him begging. "Isn't this the man who used to sit and beg?" they asked.

"It's the same man," some said.

"No," others said. "This man just looks like him."

He told them, "I'm the same man."

A Different Sort of Miracle

After Jesus had said this, He spit on the ground. He mixed it with dust and put that mud on the eyes of the blind man.
JOHN 9:6

Can you imagine what this blind man must have been thinking when Jesus spit on the ground and then put mud on his eyes? If someone did this to you, what would you think? Jesus told him to go wash his eyes in some water, and when the mud was washed away, the man could see. What an amazing miracle! Sometimes God doesn't do things the way we expect. Sometimes He surprises us. But He still loves to perform miracles!

Lord, You're always thinking of fun ways to surprise us! Your miracles are the best! Amen.

Jesus—the Good Shepherd

JOHN 10:1-39

A shepherd keeps his sheep safe in a barn. The shepherd always goes into the barn through the door. A thief sneaks into the barn another way. The shepherd knows his sheep by name, and they know his voice. They won't follow a stranger."

Jesus was explaining why the once-blind man followed Him. But the people couldn't understand His meaning. So He tried again: "This is the truth. I'm the barn door. All who came before Me are thieves. But the sheep didn't listen to them. Remember, I'm the door. Anyone who enters through Me will be saved. They'll go in and out of the pasture. The thieves come to kill. I came that people would have life, overflowing life.

"I'm the Good Shepherd. The Good Shepherd gives His life for the sheep. I know My own sheep and My sheep know Me. Just like the Father knows Me and I know My Father."

"You're only human. God isn't Your Father!" Some of the Jews picked up stones to throw at Jesus.

"I've done many of My Father's good works. Is this why you want to stone Me?" When they tried to arrest Jesus, He escaped.

Looking After His Sheep

"I am the Good Shepherd.
The Good Shepherd gives His life for the sheep."
JOHN 10:11

Did you know that Jesus is your Shepherd? It's true! You're like a little sheep in the field, wandering around without knowing where to go. Sometimes you feel lost and alone. Then the shepherd comes along and says, "Go this way! Follow me!" So you follow him and he leads you back to the fold, where all the other sheep are waiting. That's what it's like to listen for God's voice. He's such a good and loving Shepherd. He takes care of you, His baby sheep, and makes sure you are safe at all times.

Lord, thank You for being my good Shepherd! I'm so glad
You're telling me which way to go. I would
be lost without You. Amen.

The Good Samaritan

LUKE 10:30–37

The lawyer wanted to trick Jesus. He asked, "Who is my neighbor?"

Jesus answered with a story: "A man traveled from Jerusalem to Jericho. He was robbed and beaten by bandits. As he lay on the road, a priest walked right by. So did a Levite. But a Samaritan had pity. He washed and bandaged the traveler's wounds and carried him to a nearby inn. This Samaritan paid the innkeeper to care for the man.

"Which of these three was the wounded man's neighbor?"

"The man who had pity."

"Right," said Jesus. "Go and do the same."

Be Kind to Others

Then a man from the country of Samaria came by.
He went up to the man. As he saw him,
he had loving-pity on him.
LUKE 10:33

This poor man needed help! So many people walked right by him and pretended not to notice him at all. But one kind man stopped and gave him the help he needed. Maybe you know what that feels like. Maybe you tripped and skinned your knee or fell and scraped your arm. Someone came to rescue you, cleaned your wounds, and helped put on bandages. It feels good to have help when you're hurting. God wants you to help others. Be like the Good Samaritan whenever you have the chance.

Lord, I want to be a Good Samaritan.
Thanks for using me to help others. Amen.

Jesus Is the Resurrection

JOHN 11:17–53

A man named Lazarus lay sick in Bethany, Mary and Martha's village. These women sent a message to Jesus: "Lazarus is sick." But when Jesus heard this, He waited two days. When Jesus got to Bethany, Lazarus had been dead four days. Martha went out to meet Jesus while Mary stayed home. "Lord, if You'd been here," she said, "Lazarus wouldn't have died. But I know God will give You anything You ask."

"Your brother will return from death."

"I know, Lord," said Martha. "He'll come back with the resurrection on the last day."

"I am the resurrection and the life," said Jesus to Martha. "Those who believe in Me may die, but they'll live again. Do you believe this, Martha?"

"Yes, Lord," Martha replied. "I believe You're Christ, God's Son, who has come into the world." Then she hurried home.

"Lord, You should have been here," Mary wept. "Then Lazarus wouldn't have died."

Jesus began to weep. "See how much He loved Lazarus?" some said.

But others said, "He made the blind man see. Couldn't He have kept this man from dying?" These words made Jesus sad.

Lazarus's tomb was covered by a boulder. "Remove it," He said.

"Lord," complained Martha, "the body's begun to stink."

"Martha, I told you to believe and you'd see God's glory. Thank You, Father. You've heard Me." Jesus said this so the people would believe in Him. He spoke loudly: "Lazarus, come out."

Many Jews saw Lazarus come forth and believed. Others told the Pharisees, who worried, "Soon everyone will believe in Him." So they plotted to kill Jesus.

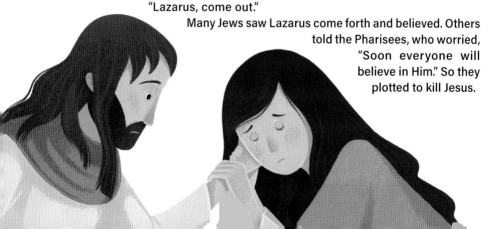

Interesting Words

Jesus said to her, "I am the One Who raises the dead and gives them life. Anyone who puts his trust in Me will live again, even if he dies."
JOHN 11:25

J esus said something very interesting to Mary: "Those who believe in Me may die, but they'll live again. Do you believe this, Martha?" It's sad to think about, but all people die. The great thing about trusting in Jesus is that we get to come alive again and live in heaven with Him. Think about the grass in your yard. It turns brown in the winter. It dies. But in the springtime it's green again. It comes back to life. That's what will happen for you if you put your faith in Jesus.

Jesus, thanks for giving me new life in heaven!
I can't wait to see it for myself. Amen.

God's Search for Sinners

Luke 15:1-24

Tax collectors and sinners gathered to hear Jesus. Pharisees and other religious people grumbled: "Jesus welcomes sinners and even eats with them."

So Jesus told them this story: "Suppose you have a hundred sheep and lose one. Don't you leave the ninety-nine to search for the lost sheep? When you find it, you return with joy. You say to your friends, 'Rejoice with me! I've found my lost sheep.' So listen to Me. There's great joy in heaven when one sinner turns away from sin. Much more than over ninety-nine law keepers like you."

Jesus thought this story would help them:

"A man had two sons. He divided his property between them. The younger son took his share and went to a faraway country. He spent everything he had there in foolish living. Then famine came to the land. With no food, he worked feeding pigs. He had to eat the pigs' food.

"At last, he started thinking sensibly. 'My father's servants have food. But here I am starving! I'm going home. I'll say, "Father, I've sinned against heaven and against you. Don't call me your son anymore. Make me one of your hired workers." '

"He set off for home. His father saw him coming. Filled with love, he ran and hugged his son. The young man said, 'Father, I've sinned against you. I shouldn't be called your son anymore.' But his father interrupted.

" 'Quickly,' the father told his servants, 'bring my best clothes for him. Put a ring on his finger and shoes on his feet. Let's eat and celebrate! My son was dead and now he's alive. He was lost and now he's found.' They began to celebrate."

God Is Searching for the Lost

"The son got up and went to his father. While he was yet a long way off, his father saw him. The father was full of loving-pity for him. He ran and threw his arms around him and kissed him."
LUKE 15:20

God is like the father in this story. He's always searching for His lost kids. Many of God's kids wander away from Him. They run away from home. But God wants them to come back. So He watches and watches, hoping they will return. If you really want to make God happy, stay close to Him. Don't wander away. Don't make Him search for you. Stick close to Him all of your life.

Lord, help me to stick close to You! I don't want to be like the prodigal son and wander away from home. I don't want You to have to search for me, Lord! Amen.

"Let the Little Children Come"

LUKE 18:15–17

Parents brought their children and tiny babies to Jesus. They only wanted Him to touch them. But then the disciples noticed what these parents were doing. They sternly ordered them to stop.

But Jesus called for them. "Let the little children come to Me. Don't stop them. The kingdom of God belongs to people like these children.

"I'll tell you the truth: You must receive the kingdom like a child. If not, you will never enter into it." Then He held the babies and gently touched the children.

Jesus Loves to Hang Out with Kids

Jesus called the followers to Him and said, "Let the little children come to Me. Do not try to stop them. The holy nation of God is made up of ones like these."
LUKE 18:16

Some people don't like to hang out with little kids. They think they're too loud. Other people think they're messy. But guess who loves hanging out with kids like you? Jesus! He says, "Come on! Spend time with Me." Doesn't that make you excited? So what does a playdate with Jesus look like? You hang out with Him, pray, sing, tell Him stories, and then listen as He whispers, "I love you, child!" Doesn't that sound great?

Thanks for hanging out with me, Jesus.
I love our times together. Amen.

"Salvation Has Come to This House"

LUKE 19:1–28

Bartimaeus and the crowd followed Jesus into Jericho. As He was passing through, more people gathered to see Him. A man was there named Zaccheus. He was a rich man because he was in charge of tax collecting. He was trying to see Jesus. But Zaccheus was too short to see over the crowd. So he ran ahead to a sycamore tree. He climbed the tree to see over the people. Jesus was going to pass that way. Jesus came there, looked up, and said, "Zaccheus, hurry down. I'm going to stay at your house today."

So Zaccheus hurried down and happily welcomed Jesus to his house. But people grumbled, "Jesus is a guest in the house of a sinner."

Zaccheus stood there in his house. "Lord," he said, "half of all I own I'll give to the poor. If I've cheated anyone, I'll pay them back four times as much."

"Today, salvation has come to this house." Jesus spoke to everyone within ear-shot. "Zaccheus is a son of Abraham just as you are. Remember, the Son of Man came to seek out and save the lost."

Jesus Loves Everyone

When Jesus came to the place, He looked up and saw
Zaccheus. He said, "Zaccheus, come down at
once. I must stay in your house today."
LUKE 19:5

Some people were mad because Jesus went to eat at Zaccheus's house. They said, "How can Jesus eat with a bad man, a sinner? Doesn't He know what Zaccheus has done?" Jesus knew, of course. He knows all things. But He loves everyone, good and bad. That's great news, because we all mess up sometimes. We all make mistakes. Doesn't it make you feel good to know that Jesus will go on loving you even if you mess things up?

Lord, I've made a lot of mistakes, but You still love me.
Thank You so much for caring about me in
good times and bad. Amen.

"Hosanna in the Highest Heaven!"

MATTHEW 21:1-11; LUKE 19:29-44

Jesus was headed for Jerusalem. He instructed two disciples, "You'll find a donkey and her colt that's never been ridden. Untie them and bring them to Me. If anyone says anything to you, say, 'The Lord needs them.' He'll send them right away."

The two disciples found the donkey just as He said. They brought him the donkey and her colt. They spread their cloaks over the animals' backs. Jesus rode the donkey from the Mount of Olives into Jerusalem.

People covered the path with their cloaks. Others spread palm leaves in the way. They praised God loudly and joyfully: "Blessed is the King who comes in the name of the Lord! Hosanna in the highest heaven!"

Jesus Was Special

The people who went in front and those who followed Jesus called out, "Greatest One! The Son of David! Great and honored is He Who comes in the name of the Lord! Greatest One in the highest heaven."
MATTHEW 21:9

How special Jesus must have felt as people ushered Him into Jerusalem like royalty! "Hosanna!" the people yelled. As He rode into town on that donkey, people must have stared, thinking He was really something special. And He was! Maybe you know what it feels like to be treated like you're special. Maybe your mom, dad, or a grandparent treats you this way sometimes. It feels great to be treated like you have value. Remember, you are created in the image of God, so you are very special indeed.

Jesus, You are so special. You're the King of kings!
Thanks for treating me like I'm special, too. Amen.

Jesus Tells of His Return

MATTHEW 25:31–46

When I come in glory, I'll sit on a glorious throne. All the nations on earth will gather there. I'll divide the people into two groups. This is like a shepherd who separates the sheep from the goats. I'll say to those on the right, 'Come here. You're blessed by My Father. Here's the kingdom He has waiting for you. I was hungry, and you gave Me food. I was thirsty, and you gave Me something to drink. When I was a stranger, you welcomed Me. I was naked, and you gave Me clothes. You visited Me in prison.'

"Those people will ask, 'When did we do these things?'

" 'Here's the truth: You did this to the smallest member of My family. So you did it to Me.'

"Then I'll speak to those on My left side. 'Get away from Me. Go to the eternal fire that's ready for the devil and his angels. You never did any of these things for Me. You did nothing for the littlest member of My family. So you never did it to Me.' "

Then Jesus told His disciples: "The Passover is in two days. Then I'll be arrested and crucified."

A Sheep or a Goat?

*"All the nations of the earth will be gathered before Him.
He will divide them from each other as a shepherd
divides the sheep from the goats."*
MATTHEW 25:32

When you hear the story of the sheep and the goats, what do you think about? Everyone wants to be a sheep, of course! A sheep is someone who takes care of others. You don't have to do big things to let others know you care. Often something as simple as a hug or a few kind words will do the trick. So who do you want to love on today? A grandparent? An elderly neighbor? Think of several creative ways you can be "sheepish."

*Lord, I want to be a sheep! I want to care about others
in fun ways. Give me great ideas, I pray. Amen.*

The Lord's Last Meal

Luke 22:7-20; Matthew 26:26-28

The Passover had come. Peter and John prepared the feast in a house in Jerusalem. Jesus and the disciples ate together in a large upstairs room. "I've been looking forward to this Passover," He said. "I want to eat this meal with you before I suffer. I'll never eat it again until the kingdom comes."

Jesus took a loaf of bread. "Take and eat this. It represents My body which is broken for you."

Then He took a cup of wine. "Take this and share it. It represents the blood which I will shed for forgiveness of sins."

A Special Meal

They went and found everything as Jesus had said.
They got ready for the special supper.
LUKE 22:13

Think about your favorite day of the year. Is it Christmas? Easter Sunday? One of the best things about special days is the mealtime. Sitting around the table with people you love is a blast. Laughing, talking, sharing stories. What fun! Jesus had a special meal with His followers, too. He showed them how to go on celebrating His life even after He was gone. Celebrating Jesus is a wonderful way to remember all He has done for us.

I love when my family comes together for a meal, Lord.
We eat, we laugh, we have lots of fun. Thanks for
giving us these special times. Amen.

Arrest in the Garden

MATTHEW 26:30-56

At a garden called Gethsemane, Jesus prayed, "My Father, don't make Me do this. But this is what You want. So I'll give up what I want."

Judas Iscariot arrived at Gethsemane. With him was a large crowd with swords and clubs. "The one I kiss is Jesus," Judas told them. "Arrest Him."

Judas quickly walked to Jesus. "Hello, Teacher!" he said, and then he kissed Him.

"Friend," said Jesus, "do what you came to do." Then He spoke to the crowd: "You've come to arrest Me with swords and clubs. Am I a bandit? I taught you every day in the temple. You didn't arrest Me there." All the disciples ran from the garden, and Jesus was led away.

Hard Things

Jesus said to him, "Friend, do what you came to do."
Then they came and put their hands on Jesus and took Him.
MATTHEW 26:50

There are so many times we have to do things we don't really feel like doing—making our bed, cleaning our room, helping to clear the table, doing our homework. It's always a good idea to obey, even if we're not in the mood. Did you know that Jesus struggled, too? In the garden, before His death, He prayed, "God, don't make Me do this!" In that very moment, He didn't want to give up His life. But aren't you glad He did it anyway? If Jesus hadn't died on the cross, then heaven would be out of our reach.

Help me to do the hard stuff,
Lord. . .even when I don't feel like it. Amen.

Guilty or Innocent?

LUKE 22:63–71; LUKE 23:1–7; JOHN 18:28–38

That night, they mocked and beat and blindfolded Jesus. The next morning, the leaders and chief priests gathered. They said, "If You are the Christ, tell us."

He replied, "If I tell you, you won't believe. If I ask you questions, you won't answer. But from now on, I'll be seated at God's throne."

They tied Jesus up and led Him away.

The priests and leaders went to Pilate's palace.

"Are You the Jews' King?" Pilate asked Jesus.

"You say I'm a king. But I came for one reason: to bring the truth."

"What is truth?" scoffed Pilate. Then he told the Jews, "This man is innocent."

But they insisted. "He upsets people everywhere, from Galilee to Jerusalem."

"Herod is in charge in Galilee," said Pilate. "Take Him to Herod."

"This Man Is Innocent"

Pilate asked Jesus, "Are You the King of the Jews?"
He said, "What you said is true."
LUKE 23:3

Do you know what it means to be innocent? It means you didn't do anything wrong. Jesus never did anything wrong in His entire life. He never messed up. He never punched His brother or told lies about His sister. He never cheated in school or gossiped behind His friend's back. Jesus lived a sinless life. Isn't it interesting that Jesus—the only person who never sinned—had to die for the sins of others? That's how much He loves us! Our precious, sinless Savior gave up His life so that we could live.

Wow, Jesus! I mess up all the time, but You never did.
Thank You for dying for my sins. I'm so grateful. Amen.

"Crucify Him! Crucify Him!"

LUKE 23:8–25

Herod was happy. He'd heard of Jesus and hoped He'd do a miracle for him. This was his chance. But Jesus didn't answer any of his questions. The leading priests kept up their complaints about Jesus. Herod and his soldiers treated Him shamefully and mocked Him. Finally, they sent Him back to Pilate. Jesus arrived wearing a royal robe. This was a joke about Jesus being King.

"This man hasn't done anything wrong," Pilate told them. "Herod doesn't seem to think so either. That's why he sent Jesus back to me. He's done nothing worth dying for. I'll just whip Him and let Him go." By this time many people had gathered.

"Away with Him!" shouted the crowd. "Let Barabbas out of prison instead." Barabbas was a murderer. But Pilate still wanted to let Jesus go. The crowd kept shouting, "Crucify Him! Crucify Him!" Pilate tried one more time, but they shouted him down. So Pilate let the murderer Barabbas out of prison. He then took Jesus, had Him whipped, and gave Him to the crowd.

Herod and Pilate had never liked each other. But the day they questioned Jesus, the two men became friends.

An Angry Crowd

Pilate wanted to let Jesus go free so he talked to them again.
But they cried out, "Nail Him to a cross! Nail Him to a cross!"
LUKE 23:20–21

⟡

Why do you suppose the crowd was so angry that day? Why did so many people yell for Jesus to be crucified? When people come together in a big mob like that, they get carried away. They go along with the group instead of thinking for themselves. That's why it's so important for you to stand up for what you believe in. Don't go along with the crowd—at school, in your neighborhood, or on the playground. When people try to make you agree with them, you don't have to. Take a stand for what's right.

⟡

I don't want to go along with the crowd, Jesus. Help me to
stick with You, even if others disagree with me. Amen.

The Death of Jesus

LUKE 23:26–43; MATTHEW 27:45–54; JOHN 19:30

They took Jesus away. The crowd made Simon of Cyrene carry Jesus' cross. Women mourned for Jesus. Two criminals were led away to die with Jesus. Jesus was crucified with a criminal on each side. The leaders made fun of Jesus. The soldiers also mocked Him by offering vinegar to drink. Even Pilate put a sign on the cross: THIS IS THE KING OF THE JEWS.

One of the crucified criminals joined the cursing, but the other criminal said, "Jesus, remember me when You come into Your kingdom."

Jesus answered, "Today you'll be with Me in Paradise."

Darkness fell as Jesus hung on the cross. Then Jesus loudly cried, "My God, My God, why have You abandoned Me?" Then He said, "It is finished," and stopped breathing. At that moment, the curtain in the temple was torn. This opened the holy of holies. An earthquake rumbled across the land, and the rocks were split.

The captain of the Roman guards saw these things and was terrified. "Absolutely, this man was God's Son," he declared.

Why Did Jesus Die?

*Jesus said to him, "For sure, I tell you,
today you will be with Me in Paradise."*
LUKE 23:43

Have you ever wondered why Jesus died on the cross for us? It's just so sad, and it doesn't seem fair, does it? Why should the good guy die for the bad guys? Jesus decided to do it this way to prove how much He loves us. Even on our worst day, when we've done something really wrong, He loves us enough to die for us. Wow! Think about the words Jesus spoke to the criminal on the cross next to Him: "Today you will be with Me in Paradise." Even when He was dying, Jesus was thinking of others.

*Thank You for thinking of me, Lord. I don't deserve it,
but I'm so grateful You died for me. Amen.*

Jesus Rises from the Dead

MATTHEW 27:57–28:7; JOHN 19:38–42; JOHN 20:1–18

Jesus' body was laid in a tomb, and a heavy rock was rolled across the tomb's door. Guards watched over the tomb.

The sun was rising Sunday morning, the third day since Jesus' death. Mary from Bethany and Mary Magdalene came to His tomb. Suddenly, an earthquake rumbled. An angel had rolled away the stone.

The angel spoke: "Don't be afraid, women. I know you're looking for Jesus. He isn't here. He's left death behind, just as He said He would. Here, look where He lay. Quickly, go tell His disciples this: Jesus is waiting for them in Galilee. Meet Him there."

Mary Magdalene stood alone, weeping by the tomb. She turned around. There was Jesus! But Mary thought He was the gardener. "Sir," she said, "have you taken away my Lord? Tell me where you've laid Him."

Jesus said to her, "Mary."

"Teacher!"

"Don't hold on to Me," He said. "I haven't yet gone up to My Father. Go and tell My brothers this: I'm going up to My Father and your Father. I'm going to My God and your God."

Mary Magdalene went and announced to the disciples, "I've seen the Lord!" She told them what had happened.

Hide-and-Seek

The angel said to the women, "Do not be afraid. I know you are looking for Jesus Who was nailed to the cross. He is not here! He has risen from the dead as He said He would. Come and see the place where the Lord lay."
MATTHEW 28:5–6

Have you ever played hide-and-seek? It's a fun game, isn't it? On the Sunday morning after Jesus died on the cross, His followers went to His tomb (the place where He was buried), but He had disappeared. Poof! The tomb was empty. Was this a game of hide-and-seek, or had something else happened? An angel spoke to the women, saying, "He's not here! He's risen from the dead!" Wow! Jesus wasn't hiding from them. He had performed the greatest miracle of all!

Thank You, Jesus, for rising from the dead. Amen!

Jesus Appears in Jerusalem

LUKE 24:28-49; JOHN 20:24-28

The two disciples didn't recognize Jesus. In Emmaus, they sat down to eat together. Jesus took the bread, blessed it, and broke it. When He gave it to them, they saw who He was. But Jesus had vanished.

They rushed back to Jerusalem and told the disciples. "Jesus has appeared to Peter, too!" they were told. Just then they were startled and terrified. Jesus Himself stood among them. "Peace be with you," He said. But they thought they were seeing a ghost.

Returning from death, Jesus stood with His disciples in Jerusalem. "Why is there doubt and fear in your hearts? Touch Me and see." The disciples were so happy but couldn't believe their eyes. "Have you anything to eat?" asked Jesus. They watched while Jesus ate.

As He opened their spiritual understanding, they heard what Moses and the prophets had written about Him. "Christ will suffer and rise from the dead, and the whole world will know it," said Jesus. "You've seen and understood all this.

"Soon I'll send you the Holy Spirit as My Father promised. Stay here in the city until power from above covers you like clothing."

The disciple named Thomas didn't see these things. He didn't believe it had happened. "I'll have to touch His wounds before I believe," he said. A week later, the doors were shut. Suddenly, Jesus stood among them.

"Reach out, Thomas," He said. "Touch My hands. Don't doubt; believe."

"My Lord and my God," answered Thomas as he touched Jesus.

Eyes of Faith

The other followers told him, "We have seen the Lord!" He said to them, "I will not believe until I see the marks made by the nails in His hands. I will not believe until I put my finger into the marks of the nails. I will not believe until I put my hand into His side."
JOHN 20:25

The disciples told Thomas that Jesus had risen from the dead, but he didn't believe it. He had to see for himself. Maybe you're like Thomas. You don't believe things until you see them with your own eyes. That's okay, but remember. . .having true faith means you believe even when you can't see. Trust God to do the impossible, even if you can't see it with your eyes.

I trust You, Lord. I don't have to see it to believe it! Amen.

Jesus Is Taken into Heaven

ACTS 1:3–11

Jesus Christ proved that He was alive many times. For forty days, He stayed with the disciples, speaking about God's kingdom. He ordered them not to leave Jerusalem. Rather, they were to wait there for the Father's promise. "I mentioned this to you before," He said. "John baptized with water. But in a few days, you'll be baptized with the Holy Spirit."

"Lord," they asked, "is now the time You'll bring the kingdom to Israel?" They were gathered together on the Mount of Olives.

"You can't know the times the Father has set for these things. But you will receive power. The Holy Spirit will come upon you like clothing. Then you'll speak for Me starting in Jerusalem. Then in Judea, Samaria, and to the ends of the earth."

After Jesus said this, He was lifted up as they watched. Then a cloud took Him out of sight. While He was going, the disciples gazed toward heaven. Two men wearing white clothes stood with them. "Men from Galilee, why are you standing there looking up? This Jesus has been taken from you into heaven. But He'll come back in the same way as you saw Him go."

Gone for a Little While

*When Jesus had said this and while they were still looking
at Him, He was taken up. A cloud carried Him
away so they could not see Him.*
ACTS 1:9

Do you know what it's like when company comes over? They stay at your house for a few days, then they have to leave to go home. You miss them so much and can't wait until the next time they come to visit. That's how it is with Jesus. He came to earth, died, then went to heaven. But He's coming back. . .this time to take people to heaven with Him. That's going to be the very best visit of all, because it will never end.

*Jesus, I'm going to get to visit with You forever in heaven.
Thanks for inviting me! Amen.*

Pentecost in Jerusalem

ACTS 2:1-39

Fifty days after Jesus was crucified, there was a big holiday. It was called Pentecost. At that time, many thousands of people visited Jerusalem. The disciples were all together that day. Suddenly, a sound like violent wind filled the house. Fire appeared and rested on each of them. They were all filled with the Holy Spirit. The Spirit made them able to speak in other languages. Then a curious crowd gathered. They were from many different nations. But they each heard the Gospel in their own language.

Peter said, "Everyone, turn from your sins, be forgiven, and be baptized in the name of Jesus Christ. You'll be given the Holy Spirit as a gift. This promise is for you, your children, and all who are far away." Three thousand people believed in Jesus that day.

When We Pray Together

"God says, 'In the last days I will send My Spirit on all men.
Then your sons and daughters will speak God's Word.
Your young men will see what God has given them
to see. Your old men will dream dreams.' "
ACTS 2:17

The disciples stuck together after Jesus went to heaven. They prayed together a lot. Did you know that exciting things happen when we pray together? It's true. The next time you have a really big prayer request, ask other people to pray with you. On the day of Pentecost, the Holy Spirit came and made quite an entrance! Lives were changed forever. That's what happens when we stick together and pray—God shows up in a mighty way!

Thanks for the reminder to pray as a team, Lord!
I can't wait to see how You show up. Amen.

Walking and Leaping and Praising God

ACTS 3:1–8

"Give me money, please," begged a disabled man near the temple. "I've been crippled since I was born." Peter and John, passing nearby, heard the man's plea.

"I have no silver or gold," Peter said to him, "but I'll give you what I have. In the name of Jesus Christ of Nazareth, stand up and walk." Peter took the man's hand and helped him up.

Instantly, the man's feet and ankles became strong. Jumping up, he walked. The man went into the temple with Peter and John. He was walking and leaping and praising God.

Celebrate Answered Prayers

Each day a certain man was carried to the Beautiful Gate of the house of God. This man had never been able to walk. He was there begging for money from those who were going in.
ACTS 3:2

This poor beggar man sat, day after day, with nothing to do but beg for money so that he could eat. When Peter came along, the man asked for money, but Peter gave him something much better. He prayed, and the man was healed. Wow! After that, the man started doing a happy dance! He couldn't help himself. He went walking and leaping and praising God! And guess what? God loved it! God loves when you celebrate answered prayers this way, too.

God, I get it! When You answer my prayers, I'm going to praise You. I don't care who hears, Lord! You are worthy of praise. Amen.

"You Lied to God!"

ACTS 4:32–5:11

With great power and with one accord, the apostles declared the Lord's resurrection. Great grace was upon them all. Those who owned houses sold them. The money was given to those who were in need.

But a man named Ananias sold some property. His wife, Sapphira, agreed that they keep some of the money. Only part of it was given for the poor.

"Ananias," said Peter, "why has Satan caused you to lie? The Holy Spirit knows you held back part of the money. When you sold the land, the money was yours. Now, you have lied to God!"

Hearing this, Ananias fell down and died. Young men took the body out for burial. Later, Ananias's wife came in. She didn't know what had happened. "Did you and your husband sell your land?" asked Peter.

"Yes," Sapphira answered.

"Why did you test the Lord's Spirit? There are the men who buried your husband. They're ready to carry you out." Immediately, she fell to the floor, dead. Sapphira was buried beside her husband. And the fear of God came over the whole church.

Don't Lie to God

A man by the name of Ananias and his wife,
Sapphira, sold some land.
ACTS **5:1**

Why do you suppose God was so angry with Ananias and Sapphira? Was it because of the amount of money they gave? No, not at all! He was mad because they lied. They told Peter and the others that they had given *all* of their money, but really they had given only part of it. They lied to make themselves look more generous. But God saw the truth. Did you know that the Lord sees whenever we lie? It's true! He wants you to be a truth teller, even when it's really hard. So speak up! Tell the truth.

I want to be a truth teller, Lord!
Help me not to lie to others or to You. Amen.

A Man Full of Faith

ACTS 6:1–15

God's Word kept on spreading in Jerusalem. The number of disciples grew larger. Even a great many priests came to faith in Christ.

Seven men were chosen from among the believers. They were full of the Holy Spirit and wisdom. Their job was to care for the sharing of food among the believers. One of these was Stephen, a man full of faith, grace, and power. He did great wonders and signs among the people. Some among the Jews rose up and argued with Stephen. But they couldn't stand against his wisdom and spirit. So they secretly paid people to accuse him: "We've heard Stephen say terrible things against Moses and God." The people, leaders, and teachers of Moses' law were all angry.

Stephen was forced to go in to the council of rulers. There people lied about him. "He says Jesus of Nazareth will destroy the temple," they said. "He wants to change the traditions that Moses gave us."

The high priest looked at Stephen. "Are these things true?" he asked. The whole council also looked deeply into Stephen's face. They saw that it was like the face of an angel.

An Unpopular Message

Stephen was a man full of faith and power.
He did many great things among the people.
ACTS 6:8

Stephen couldn't help himself. He had to speak the message of Jesus Christ. It wasn't a popular message with the people of his day, but he spoke up anyway. Did you know that God wants you to speak up, to tell others about Jesus? Even if it's really hard, do it anyway. Even if people think you're crazy for believing in Jesus, tell others anyway. When you have the faith and power that Stephen had, you're bold. You can share the Good News straight from your heart.

Lord, I want to have the courage of Stephen. When people ask
me questions about You, I want to speak with
boldness. Help me, I pray. Amen.

Stephen Is Stoned to Death

ACTS 7:2-60

Stephen gave the council a meaningful speech. Beginning from Abraham, he traced the history of the Jewish people. But the council became enraged. "Your ancestors persecuted every prophet," Stephen said. "These prophets predicted that Christ would come—and now you're His murderers." With a shout, they rushed him. "Look," Stephen said, "the heavens are opened. There's Jesus standing next to God." They covered their ears and dragged him from Jerusalem. There Stephen was stoned to death. "Lord Jesus, receive my spirit," he prayed. Then he knelt, saying, "Don't hold this sin against them." And Stephen died.

The Heavens Opened

While they threw stones at Stephen, he prayed,
"Lord Jesus, receive my spirit."
ACTS 7:59

M ost people don't like to think about death. They think it's going to be scary or sad. But when you look at Stephen's story, you see something interesting. Just as Stephen was dying, God opened the curtain of heaven and gave him a sneak peek! What did Stephen see? He saw Jesus standing next to God. Many people have claimed to have had sneak peeks of heaven. They tell of marvelous things. What do you think heaven will be like?

Lord, sometimes I wonder what heaven will be like. I know there are
streets of gold and gates of pearl. Best of all, I know You're there.
One day I'll see it all for myself. Thank You, Lord. Amen.

Saul—Blinded by the Light

Acts 9:1–10

A young man named Saul approved of Stephen's death. Then Saul began to run the believers out of Jerusalem. He breathed threats and murder against the disciples. Saul went to the high priest for permission to go to Damascus. He planned to arrest men and women who followed Jesus' way. When Saul came near Damascus, a light from heaven flashed around him. He fell to the ground. A voice said, "Saul, Saul, why do you persecute Me?"

"Who are You, Lord?" asked Saul.

"I'm Jesus, the One you're harassing."

Saul lay on the ground, blinded by a light from heaven. Jesus Himself spoke: "Get up and go into the city. There you'll be told what to do." The men traveling with Saul were standing speechless. They heard the voice but saw no one. They led Saul by the hand into Damascus. For three days, Saul was blind and ate nothing.

Then the Lord spoke to a disciple named Ananias. "A man from Tarsus named Saul has seen a vision. In it, you, Ananias, touch him so he can see again. Go and do this."

"Lord," Ananias said, "I've heard of this man. He's done so much evil to Your saints in Jerusalem. He's come here to arrest people who call on Your name."

"Go, Ananias. I've chosen Saul to bring My name to people of all nations. He'll bring My name to kings and the people of Israel. I will personally teach him how much he must suffer. This suffering will be for My name."

Ananias went. "Brother Saul," he said, "the Lord Jesus has sent me. Receive your sight. Be filled with the Holy Spirit." Instantly, Saul could see again. He was baptized, ate a meal, and got his strength back.

Join God's Team

He fell to the ground. Then he heard a voice say, "Saul, Saul, why are you working so hard against Me?"
ACTS 9:4

Wow, Saul has an amazing story, doesn't he? There he was, walking down the road, when all of a sudden, he was blinded by a bright light. God had a talk with him, and before long, Saul was a believer. Before he met up with God that day, Saul was working against God. He was treating Christians badly. After the Lord saved him, Saul became a great preacher, telling everyone about Jesus. It's always better to be on God's team. What about you? Are you on God's team?

God, I'm going to stay on Your team forever. I want to tell others about You so they can be on Your team, too! Amen.

Saul—the Preacher of Jesus

Acts 9:20-31

Saul stayed for several days with the disciples in Damascus. Immediately, he went to the Jewish synagogues. "Jesus is the Son of God," he declared.

"Isn't this the man who made havoc in the church in Jerusalem?" After a while, some people plotted to kill Saul. But Saul found out. The gates were watched day and night. So the disciples brought him to a hole in the city's wall. They lowered Saul down in a basket, and he escaped.

Saul returned to Jerusalem. He tried to join the disciples there. But they were afraid. "He doesn't believe in Jesus," they said. But a disciple named Barnabas introduced Saul to the apostles. Barnabas told them how Saul had seen the Lord.

"The Lord spoke to him in Damascus," said Barnabas. "And Saul boldly preached the Gospel there." So Saul stayed with the church in Jerusalem. He spoke and argued with the Greek Jews, but they plotted to kill him. So the believers put Saul on a boat in Caesarea. From there, he sailed home to Tarsus.

And the whole church had peace and was built up.

People Can Change

At once Saul began to preach in the Jewish places
of worship that Jesus is the Son of God.
ACTS 9:20

Did you know that people can change? Bad people can become good, with God's help. Even the meanest person you know can change, if he asks Jesus to come and live inside his heart. When someone we know changes, we might have trouble trusting them at first. Sometimes we just remember the bad things they did. But God used Saul's story to teach us that He can change people from the inside out, and we can trust in His good work. Are there any areas of your life that need changing today? Don't be afraid to ask God to change your heart, too.

I'm so glad You're a God who changes people.
I trust in Your perfect power, Lord. Amen.

Peter's Vision in Joppa

Acts 10:1-23

In Caesarea lived a Roman soldier named Cornelius. So Cornelius wasn't a Jew. He was a Gentile. Yet he was true to God and gave to the poor. He always prayed. One afternoon, this man had a vision. An angel came and said, "Cornelius?"

"What is it, Lord?" Cornelius stared at the angel in terror.

"Send men to Joppa and find Peter at Simon's house." Quickly, Cornelius sent for Peter.

About noon the next day, Peter went to Simon's roof to pray. While he waited, Peter fell into a trance. He saw a large sheet coming from heaven. In it were all kinds of animals. A voice spoke: "Peter, get up and eat these animals." But the animals in the sheet were banned by Jewish law. So, to Peter, the meat wasn't clean.

"No, Lord," said Peter. "I've never eaten any unclean meat."

"God has made this meat clean. Don't call it unclean again." Peter was puzzled about this. Just then the men came from Cornelius. The next day, Peter went with them to Cornelius's house in Caesarea.

God Loves Everyone

The voice said the second time,
"What God has made clean you must not say is unclean."
ACTS 10:15

The Jews had one way of eating, and the Gentiles had another way of eating. But God showed Peter that they could come together, in spite of their differences, because God was going to make the meat clean. Do you ever think about people who are different from you? Maybe those with a different skin color, or people who are from a different country. Did you know that God loves them just as much as He loves you? They have different customs and languages. They even eat different foods. But to God, we're all one big happy family.

God, thank You for bringing us all together and making us a family.
I'm so glad You love all the children of the world. Amen.

The Believers Are Called Christians

ACTS 11:19–30

When Stephen was killed, believers scattered all over the Middle East. In Antioch, some told the Greeks the Good News of Jesus. A great number of Gentiles became believers and turned to the Lord.

The church in Jerusalem heard of this. They sent Barnabas to Antioch. There he saw God's grace among the people. Barnabas rejoiced. "Be faithful to the Lord," he told them. "Stay devoted to Him." Barnabas was a good man, full of the Holy Spirit and faith. A great many people were brought to the Lord.

Then Barnabas went to Tarsus to look for Saul. He found him and brought him back to Antioch. For an entire year, they met with the church. Barnabas and Saul taught many, many people. The believers there were not at all like Jews. And they'd changed in ways that made them unlike Gentiles. So it was in Antioch that believers were first called Christians.

At that time, a famine came. Believers in Judea suffered without food. So the church in Antioch sent Barnabas and Saul. They brought aid to the churches in Judea.

Call Me a Christian

The followers were first called Christians in Antioch.
ACTS 11:26

❦

Believers in Jesus Christ were first called Christians in a town called Antioch. What does the word *Christian* mean? A Christian is someone who puts their faith and belief in Jesus Christ. Some people say the word means "little Christ." Think about that for a minute. From the time you put your trust in Jesus, He calls you His! You're part of His family, the family of believers, also known as Christians. There are millions of Christians around this world, so your family is very, very large indeed!

❦

Lord, I'm so happy to be a Christian. I put my faith and my trust in You, Jesus! Thanks for making me part of such a great family. Amen.

The Apostles Are Sent Out

Acts 13:1–12

Now in the church at Antioch there were prophets and teachers. They prayed together, worshiping God. The Holy Spirit said to them, "Set aside Barnabas and Saul. I've called them for My work." The leaders of the church prayed and laid their hands on them. The Holy Spirit sent Barnabas and Saul out. They took Mark and set off. The three apostles sailed to the island of Cyprus. There they spoke God's Word in the Jewish synagogues.

They traveled through the whole island. At Paphos lived a magician, a false prophet named Bar-Jesus. The ruler of Cyprus, Sergius Paulus, wanted to hear God's Word. But the magician tried to turn him away from the faith. Saul, now called Paul, watched him carefully. Paul was filled with the Holy Spirit. "You son of the devil," he said, "you enemy of all that's right, stop making the Lord's straight paths crooked. God's hand is against you. You'll not be able to see for a while." Shortly, the magician could only see darkness. He had to have someone lead him by the hand. Sergius Paulus saw this and believed. He was delighted at the teaching about the Lord.

Set Aside

While they were worshiping the Lord and eating no food so they could pray better, the Holy Spirit said, "Let Barnabas and Saul be given to Me for the work I have called them to."
ACTS 13:2

Did you know that God sets aside some people to do great things for Him? It's true. You might wonder why some people feel called to be pastors or teachers. It's because God has set them aside for this work by putting in motion a special plan for their lives. When God gives you a special calling, it's not because you're more talented or worthier than others. It's because He knows He can trust you. When you put your whole trust in God, He uses you to do amazing things!

I put my trust in You, Lord! Use me to do great things, not just when I'm grown up, but even now, Lord. Amen.

"We're Saved through Grace"

ACTS 14:27–15:1–21

The Antioch church rejoiced. God had opened the door of faith for the Gentiles! But then some people came to Antioch from Judea. They said, "You Gentile Christians must keep Moses' law."

But Paul and Barnabas said, "God is happy that the Gentiles have believed in Jesus. They don't have to do anything else to be saved." So the apostles and leaders called a meeting in Jerusalem. Paul and Barnabas went there to discuss this important problem.

The first person to speak was Peter. "Brothers, God gave the Gentiles the Holy Spirit. I was at Cornelius's house when it happened. So God must not see a difference between them and us. Anyway, no one has ever been able to keep Moses' law. We're saved through the grace of the Lord Jesus. So are the Gentiles."

Paul and Barnabas then told of the wonders God did among the Gentiles. James had the final word: "God wants to make the Gentiles into a people for His name. Let's not trouble those who are turning to God."

Saved by Grace

"We believe it is by the loving-favor of the Lord Jesus that we are saved. They are saved from the punishment of sin the same way."
ACTS 15:11

In Old Testament times, the Jewish people had to follow the Law. It was a list of very hard rules that were almost impossible to obey. (Have you ever been given hard rules? If so, then you know how tough it can be to get everything right.) Some of the Christians thought these rules should apply to everyone, but Paul and Barnabas disagreed. They knew that God's plan was about grace and forgiveness, not rules. Does this mean you should break the rules? No! But it means that God's grace is the most important thing.

I want to live my life for You, but I know I'll mess up at times. Thanks for Your grace, God. Amen.

A Speech in the Streets

Acts 22:2–22

The angry crowd heard their own language and stopped to listen. "I'm a Jew, born in Tarsus," Paul said. "But here in Jerusalem, I learned our ancestors' law. When the time came, I fought against the Christians. The high priest and elders can tell you this.

"They sent me to Damascus to arrest Christians there. On the way, about noon, a great light from heaven flashed. I fell to the ground. A voice said, 'Saul, Saul, why are you fighting Me?'

" 'Who are You, Lord?' I asked.

" 'I'm Jesus of Nazareth.'

"In the city, a good Jewish man named Ananias met me. 'God has chosen you,' he said. 'You'll tell the world of what you've seen and heard. Now get up and be baptized, calling on His name.'

"I came back here and was praying in the temple. The Lord appeared. 'Get out of this city,' He said. 'The people won't listen to you.'

" 'But Lord, I agreed when they killed Stephen,' I reasoned.

" 'Go; I am sending you far away to the Gentiles.' "

When they heard the word *Gentiles*, the crowd erupted with violent anger.

Paul Tells His Story

They listened to him until he said that. Then they all cried out with loud voices, "Kill him! Take such a man from the earth! He should not live!"
ACTS 22:22

Have you ever heard the word *testimony*? Your testimony is your story. Paul had an amazing testimony. He was once a very bad man who hated Christians. Then, after he met God on the road to Damascus, all of that changed. He became a good man. Paul shared his story everywhere he went. He told other people about the great and wonderful things God had done in his life. God wants you to share your story, too. When He does something amazing for someone you love, share the story with others so that they can know about Him, too.

I'll tell my story, Lord! I want others to know about You. Amen.

The King Hears the Gospel

Acts 25:13–19; Acts 26:20–32

Agrippa, the king of Galilee, and his wife, Bernice, visited Festus in Caesarea. "I'd like to hear this man Paul myself," said Agrippa.

"Tomorrow," agreed Festus, "you'll hear him."

The next day, King Agrippa and Bernice were escorted by military leaders and city rulers. "King Agrippa," Festus announced, "here is the man I mentioned. People claim that he should die. But he has done no wrong."

The king spoke to Paul: "You have my permission to speak."

"I'm glad to tell you my story, King Agrippa," Paul began. "You know the Jewish customs and matters of their law. Please listen patiently. I'm on trial because I believe God's promise to our ancestors. All the Jews hope for this, as well. It is that God will bring us back from death. Yet now they accuse me because I believe this!

"I hated the name of Jesus. I was furious and punished Christians. I even traveled to faraway places to arrest them." Paul described what happened to him at Damascus. He told the king of his heavenly vision.

" 'Change your mind! Turn to God!' I declared this wherever I went. I told Jews and Gentiles.

"That's why the Jews tried to kill me. But God has helped me. My message is the same as Moses and the prophets: Christ would suffer; He would be first to return from death; He would give light to all people."

"You're out of your mind, Paul!" exclaimed Festus.

"This is the levelheaded truth," said Paul.

"Do you want me to be a Christian?" asked Agrippa.

"I want you all to be like me—except without these chains."

Almost, but Not Quite

Then Agrippa said to Paul, "In this short time you have almost proven to me that I should become a Christian!"
ACTS 26:28

⁂

After King Agrippa heard Paul's story, he almost decided to believe in Jesus. . .but didn't carry through. Have you ever "almost" decided something, but changed your mind? Maybe you "almost" decided to clean your room, but changed your mind at the last minute. When it comes to trusting in the Lord, we need to go all the way. No turning back. No "almost." God wants us to give Him our whole heart. He wants us to be completely devoted to Him. Have you given the Lord your whole heart?

⁂

No "almost" for me, Lord! I'm going to believe in You 100 percent. Today I give You my whole heart, Father. No turning back. Amen.

Paul's Perilous Voyage: Part 1

Acts 26:30–27:11

"This man has done nothing wrong," the king said as he left. "He could have been set free. But now he has to take his case to the emperor."

Paul, Luke, and Aristarchus traveled to Rome with several other prisoners. They set sail with the Roman centurion Julius in charge.

From Caesarea, the ship sailed north along the coast of Judea. They anchored at Sidon. There Julius allowed Paul to visit his friends. The ship left the next day. It didn't land again until reaching Myra in Lycia. There the prisoners were moved to a ship from Alexandria. It was carrying wheat from Egypt to Italy.

Sailing was slow because the wind was blowing the wrong way. Finally, they came under the south side of the island of Crete. There they entered the port of Fair Havens. They had lost many days getting this far in the voyage. Winter would have to pass before they could sail on to Italy.

Paul spoke to the ship's captain and her owner: "I can see that this will be a dangerous voyage. The cargo will be lost, and so will our lives." But they paid no attention.

A Hard Journey

The wind was against us, and we did not sail very fast.
Then we came to a place called Fair Havens.
It was near the city of Lasea.
ACTS 27:8

The ship that Paul was on got caught in strong winds. *Whoosh! Whoosh! Whoosh!* Those crazy winds made it difficult for the ship to travel to its destination. They lost many days. Sometimes things happen in life that make things difficult. People get sick. Mothers and fathers lose jobs. People have arguments. Not everything is easy. *Whoosh! Whoosh! Whoosh!* The crazy winds blow. But God wants you to sail on, even when the winds are against you. He will bring you safely to shore if you don't give up.

I won't give up, Lord. Even during the hard times,
I will keep on trusting You. Please help me, I pray. Amen.

Paul's Perilous Voyage: Part 2

ACTS 27:12-32

Fair Havens wasn't a good place to spend the winter. "Let's take a chance and put out to sea," the captain said. They drew in the anchor and set sail close to shore. Soon a violent wind rushed down from Crete.

The storm pounded violently. All hope was lost.

Paul spoke to everyone: "Last night, an angel from my God stood by me. He said, 'Don't be afraid, Paul. You must speak to the emperor in Rome. God has granted safety to those who are sailing with you.' So keep up your courage. I have faith in God. It will be just as I've been told."

Total Darkness

We did not see the sun or stars for many days. A very bad storm kept beating against us. We lost all hope of being saved.
ACTS **27:20**

Poor Paul! He went through so much. First the winds tossed the ship around; then they got caught in a terrible storm. It was so bad that they couldn't even see the sun or stars. If you've ever been in a room at night with the lights off, you know how scary that can be. But here's the truth: God is with you, even in the darkness. When you can't see, He can. He has twenty-twenty night vision and is watching over you, even in the dark. You never have to be afraid, because God will never leave you.

I'm so glad You watch over me at night, Lord. Even when it's dark, I don't have to be afraid. Thank You, Father! Amen.

Shipwrecked on Malta

ACTS 27:39–44

It was just before dawn on the storm-tossed ship. "We've not eaten for two weeks," said Paul. "Please, have some food. It will help you to survive." Everyone watched Paul. He took bread, gave thanks to God, broke it, and began to eat. Then all 276 people in the ship took food.

Everyone ate and was satisfied. Then they threw the wheat into the sea. This made the ship float higher in the water.

When daylight broke, they could see land. There was a bay with a beach. "Run the ship aground at that beach," ordered the captain. Anchors were cast off into the sea. Steering oars were untied, ready to use. The foresail was raised, and they made for the beach. But before the ship hit the sand, it struck an underwater reef. The vessel was stuck. Its stern, pounded by waves, broke up. Danger was all around.

The soldiers said, "Let's kill the prisoners or they'll escape." But Julius wanted to save Paul and wouldn't allow this.

"If you can swim, jump overboard!" ordered the captain. The others came ashore floating on pieces of the ship. Everyone was brought safely to land.

A Shipwreck

But the captain wanted to save Paul. He kept them
from their plan. Calling out to those who could swim,
he told them to jump into the sea and swim to shore.
ACTS **27:43**

Crash! Bang! Paul's ship smashed into a reef and began to break apart. People started jumping overboard. Whew! What a crazy ending to a dangerous voyage. Here's the exciting part: The captain cared about Paul, even though Paul was a prisoner. He made sure Paul was safe. Did you know that God is like the captain of a ship? He cares about every passenger on board and wants to make sure everyone arrives safely to their destination, heaven. You can trust your Captain all the way.

I trust in You, Lord. You won't let me sink.
Thanks for taking such good care of me. Amen.

Paul Arrives in Rome

Acts 28:1-23

Paul's ship wrecked on a little island named Malta. The kind natives built a fire for the cold, wet survivors. Paul brought some brushwood to the fire. Suddenly, a snake in the brushwood bit Paul. But he shook it off into the fire. They expected Paul to drop dead. Nothing happened.

The superstitious natives thought this meant Paul was a god.

The father of a Maltese nobleman named Publius lay sick. Paul put his hands on the man and prayed. He was cured. All the people on the island then brought their sick to Paul. They also were cured.

Three months later, they set sail on a ship called the *Twin Brothers.* Sailing in front of a south wind, the apostle finally landed in Italy. Believers from Rome walked fifty miles down the Italian coast to greet Paul. He gratefully thanked God for them.

In Rome, Paul lived in his own house with a guard. The Jewish leaders visited Paul. "We've heard bad things about the Christians," they said. "But we'd like to know what you have to say." They set a day to meet with him.

A Difference Maker

When we got to Rome, Paul was allowed to live where he wanted to. But a soldier was always by his side to watch him.
ACTS 28:16

Paul went on a lot of journeys, didn't he? Wherever he went, he told people about Jesus. He prayed for the sick and they were healed. In other words, he made a difference. What about you? Do you plan to travel when you're older? Where are some of the places you hope to go? Remember, you don't have to wait until then to make a difference in the lives of the people around you. What are some things you can do right now to brighten people's lives?

Lord, thanks for showing me that I can make a difference. I don't have to wait until I'm grown, either. With Your help, I can start right now. Amen.

Salvation Is Sent to the Gentiles

Many Jewish leaders from Rome listened to Paul, morning to evening. By the day's end, they were arguing among themselves.

"The Holy Spirit was right," Paul said. "He said this to your ancestors: 'They'll listen but won't catch My meaning. They'll see but won't understand. Your words will do them no good.

They won't use their eyes to look. They won't use their ears to hear. They won't understand with their minds, turn to Me, and be healed.'

"So I want you to know this: God's salvation has been sent to the Gentiles. They'll listen."

No Discrimination

*"I want you to know that the Good News of God of knowing how
to be saved from the punishment of sin has been sent to the
people who are not Jews. And they will listen to it!"*
ACTS 28:28

Some people used to think that God only loved a few people, not all people. But here's the truth: He doesn't discriminate. He doesn't treat some people better than others. What about you? Do you treat some people better than others? God wants you to love all people the same—no matter what they look like, which language they speak, or how they dress. Love is the best gift you can give.

*Lord, thank You for reminding me that I should love all people.
I see people who look different all the time, but I won't treat
them differently. Help me to love everyone the
same, just like You do! Amen.*

John's Vision of Jesus Christ: Part 1

REVELATION 1:9–13

I was in the Spirit on the Lord's day." These words were written by the apostle John. He was a very old man. John continued, "Behind me, I heard a loud voice like a trumpet." John was in prison because he spoke God's Word. His prison was on a lonely island called Patmos. He was the last of the disciples who had walked with Jesus.

"I turned to look when I heard the voice," John wrote. "There, walking among seven gold lampstands, was Jesus Christ." John had last seen Jesus sixty years before when Jesus came back from death.

A Special Visit

I turned around to see who was speaking to me.
As I turned, I saw seven lights made of gold.
REVELATION 1:12

Jesus loves when we pray and spend time with Him. Sometimes, when He feels like surprising us, Jesus reveals Himself in special ways. He came to John for a surprise visit. Can you imagine how excited John must have been? It was the first time he had seen his friend Jesus in sixty years! He was very surprised! How excited would you be if Jesus appeared right in front of you? No doubt you would remember that special visit for the rest of your life!

Lord, one day I'm going to live in heaven with You and I'll see You all the time. Until then, I'll keep praying and spending time with You. I love our special visits! Amen.

John's Vision of Jesus Christ: Part 2

REVELATION 1:13-20

John saw Jesus Christ walking among the lampstands. Christ was wearing a long robe with a golden sash across His chest. His hair was as white as snow. His eyes were like flaming fire. His feet shone like polished brass in a furnace. His voice was like the sound of many rushing streams of water.

John saw seven stars in Christ's right hand. Out of His mouth came a sharp sword. His face was like the sun shining with full force. "I fell at His feet," John said, "like I was dead. But His hand touched me. 'Don't be afraid,' Christ said. 'I'm the first and the last. I'm the living One. I was dead, and look, I am alive forever and ever.'

"Then Christ said to me, 'Write down what I'll show you. Send the book to the seven churches in Asia. These seven stars are the angels of the seven churches. These gold lampstands are the seven churches.' "

John wrote a great book called the book of Revelation. This book includes letters to the Christian churches. It also tells of the end of time. Finally, Revelation shows us what eternity with God is like.

What Is Heaven Like?

When I saw Him, I fell down at His feet like a dead man.
He laid His right hand on me and said, "Do not
be afraid. I am the First and the Last."
REVELATION 1:17

Have you ever wondered what heaven will be like? What kind of music will we hear? What will the people look like? What will eternity with Jesus be like? John had a sneak peek! He saw glimpses of heaven while he was still alive. He saw Jesus wearing a long robe with a golden sash. His hair was as white as snow and His feet as shiny as brass. John fell at Jesus' feet, overwhelmed. What will you do when you see Jesus face-to-face?

Lord, I'll get to see You face-to-face one day.
Thank You for inviting me to live in heaven with You. Amen.

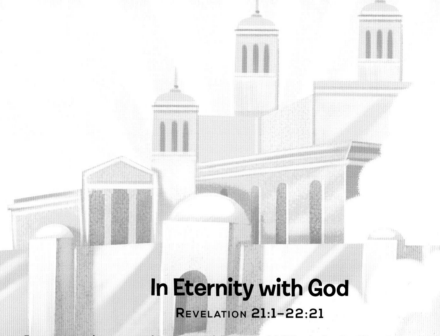

In Eternity with God
REVELATION 21:1–22:21

I saw a new heaven and a new earth," John said. "The holy city, New Jerusalem, came from heaven like a bride dressed for her husband.

"A loud voice came from God's throne. The voice said, 'God's home is with humanity. He'll dwell with them; they'll be His people. God will wipe every tear from their eyes. Death will be no more. Grief, crying, and pain will be gone. Old things are passed away. I'm making everything new.'

"New Jerusalem has God's glory. It is green like jasper, clear as crystal. The twelve gates are named for Israel's twelve tribes. Each gate is a pearl. The twelve foundations are named for the Lamb's twelve apostles. These foundations are built of precious, colorful stones.

"Its one street is pure gold, transparent as glass. Out of God's throne flows the river of the water of life. The tree of life grows on the river's banks. Its leaves heal the nations.

"Then Jesus said, 'The Spirit and the bride say come. Anyone who wishes may freely drink the water of life.'"

No More Crying, No More Pain

I saw the Holy City, the new Jerusalem. It was coming
down out of heaven from God. It was made ready
like a bride is made ready for her husband.
REVELATION 21:2

Have you ever stubbed your toe or fallen and scraped your knee? It's no fun, being hurt. Sometimes you just can't help it. . .you start crying. Life is filled with many sad and hurtful things. Many times, tears will come. But, guess what? When we get to heaven, there will be no more tears. All sadness and pain will be washed away. Can you imagine how wonderful that will be? Praise the Lord! We'll live forever with our Savior, free at last!

Lord, heaven sounds so wonderful. Thank You for taking
away my pain and my tears forever. I can't wait
to spend eternity with You! Amen.

Enjoy Even More Fantastic Bedtime Bible Stories with. . .

365 Classic Bedtime Bible Stories

365 read-aloud classic Bible stories come to life for impressionable young hearts. Beginning with the creation story, "God Creates the Earth," and ending with "In Eternity with God," children will develop faith in an almighty God who is the same yesterday, today, and forever, while journeying alongside Bible characters like Samuel, Jonah, Esther, David, John the Baptist, Mary, Joseph, and many more. *365 Classic Bedtime Bible Stories* promises to make bedtime reading a delightful learning and faith-building experience!

Hardback / 978-1-63058-380-4 / $19.99